WORLD WITHOUT END

WORLD WITHOUT END

THOMAS KEATING OCSO
and JOSEPH BOYLE OCSO

with

LUCETTE VERBOVEN

BLOOMSBURY
LONDON · OXFORD · NEW YORK · NEW DELHI · SYDNEY

Bloomsbury Continuum
An imprint of Bloomsbury Publishing Plc

50 Bedford Square
London
WCIB 3DP
UK

1385 Broadway
New York
NY 10018
USA

www.bloomsbury.com

Bloomsbury, Continuum and the Diana logo are trademarks of
Bloomsbury Publishing Plc

First published 2017

British Library Cataloguing-in-Publication Data
A catalogue record for this book is available from the British Library.

Library of Congress Cataloguing-in-Publication data has been applied for.

ISBN: PB: 9781472942487
EPDF: 9781472942463
EPUB: 9781472942494

2 4 6 8 10 9 7 5 3 1

Typeset by Newgen Knowledge Works (P) Ltd., Chennai, India
Printed and bound in Great Britain by CPI Group (UK) Ltd, Croydon CRO 4YY

MIX
Paper from
responsible sources
FSC® C020471

To find out more about our authors and books visit www.bloomsbury.com.
Here you will find extracts, author interviews, details of forthcoming
events and the option to sign up for our newsletters.

To my husband: companion, lover, soulmate

Lucette Verboven

'Once you have been born into this world
you never die'

Thomas Keating

CONTENTS

PART ONE

Introduction

A Journey

> Love bade me welcome: yet my soul drew back,
> Guilty of dust and sin.[1]

'HOW MUCH OF GOD'S reality can you accept at this point?' The monk sitting before me gazes at me with piercing eyes. Gently, though unwaveringly, he puts the awkward question right in front of me. It hits me unexpectedly because it leads me with terrifying directness to God and to myself.

I think about my life's story of rejecting and accepting God and going through this track back and forth multiple times. Is this monk, clad in black and white garb, directing the question really towards me, 'I, the unkind, ungrateful'? This line from my favourite poem *Love* by George Herbert invades my mind and makes the monk's question even more poignant. And I wonder: what do I do when Love bids me welcome? Does my soul draw back? Is it guilty of dust and sin? George Herbert, this most skilful of British poets, answers affirmatively. Definitely, your soul is guilty, he tells me, and I confirm his words for myself. But Love answers that it doesn't matter. This understanding monk tells me the same: 'You can't go wrong in this life if you trust God. It doesn't matter what you have done. God is eager to give you everything He can give you. He even makes amends to the people you may have injured.'

I had been intrigued for years by the monk who is now sitting before me and who gently but firmly answers my questions. When he mentions familiar names like Augustine, Teresa of Avila, John of the Cross, Gregory of Nyssa, I feel as if we belong to the same 'invisible band of companions' that Meister Eckhart speaks of: 'people, who are often not known to one another because they live in a remote space or time from each other but who form a kind of spiritual kinship'.[2]

Some fifteen years ago, I started travelling the world with a camera team to make an international television series for Belgium and the Netherlands. From Japan to Brazil, I met wonderful men and women, theologians, artists, politicians, philosophers, authors and scientists, and asked them about their views in an ever changing world.[3] The wise monk who is now intent on answering my questions was one of the 'wanted' guests on my list. I even contacted St Benedict's Monastery in Snowmass to ask him for an interview. But suddenly the series was cut short, in a television landscape that is growing dim and superficial.

So, I forgot about him.

Is the soul guilty? The question kept intriguing me. The soul is hard to find on lawyers' desks or in our bank accounts but still perseveres in literature. The American poet H. W. Longfellow writes that the soul of man is audible, not visible. But how can the soul be heard? Father Thomas answers: 'Silence is the language of God, all the rest is a bad translation.' I would add one exception: music! The English eminent intellectual of his time, Aldous Huxley, agrees: 'After silence

4

that which comes nearest to expressing the inexpressible is music.'[4]

I took Huxley's advice seriously and in the course of time I added musicians and composers to my guest list. Musicians were indeed most at ease when talking about the soul and the transcendent. A story about how treacherous words can be was invoked by the Catalan viol player and conductor Jordi Savall. 'At the beginning of creation, music and words were intertwined. One day, someone told a lie. Because music cannot bear lies, it dissociated itself from the word and the two became separate. This sad situation continued for a very long time. One day, someone found a way to reconcile the two, namely by praying to God. In this way Gregorian chant was created.'[5] The authentic dimension of music shines brilliantly in this story. If we converse with one another, our words may contain lies. If we sing, everybody can tell whether we are true to our being or not. Music is the most direct and deepest language to express the spiritual dimension that is so badly needed in our world. Maestro Jordi Savall concluded: '*Music cannot lie, as words can.*' Is that why chant and liturgy are intertwined in the monastery? Is that why monks in the old days were restricted to using a sign language, avoiding words, but could sing freely?

The question whether the soul is guilty kept popping up in my mind. Is it really guilty? Does it need saving? Then the famous English composer Sir John Tavener whose 'Song for Athene'[6] was played at the funeral of Princess Diana, answered me: 'I compose in order to save my soul. It has to be saved as the great writer Dante also knew. He too wrote his "Divina Commedia" in order to save his soul.'[7]

But as I discovered over the years, the notion of the soul was disappearing rapidly from modern language and society. The soul no longer has wings, as Plato once said. Whenever the subject did come up in conversations, it was met with a pitiable glance.

So, I forgot about it.

> But quick-eyed Love, observing me grow slack[8]
> From my first entrance in,
> Drew nearer to me, sweetly questioning
> If I lacked anything.[9]

However, in some strange way neither the Trappist monk whom I had forgotten nor the concept of the soul left my mind entirely. Old thoughts kept coming back and forced themselves upon me, gently reminding me that they didn't want to sink into oblivion and, in doing so, transformed themselves into new thoughts.[10] When Catholic television in Flanders, Belgium, was notified it would be closed down, I had one more interview to go. The wise but almost forgotten monk suddenly came to my mind. Wasn't his name *Father Thomas Keating*, a Trappist monk living in America, a kindred spirit to Thomas Merton?

I found out that he had become a leading figure in the rediscovery of the Christian contemplative tradition, a spiritual guide and founder of the organization, Contemplative Outreach. He had conversed with spiritual leaders of all religions and had travelled the world in order to spread the message of Centering Prayer, which he had developed with his fellow Trappist monks, Father William Meninger and Father Basil Pennington. Did he still live in the same monastery in Snowmass, Colorado?

I started devouring his books. The concept of the soul propelled itself to the fore when I read his words: 'The purpose of our historical lifetime is to provide us with the time and space for the integration and the transformation of body, soul and spirit.' And once again, after fifteen years, I phoned the monastery. The kind voice of Father Thomas Keating answered me that he would be delighted to give an interview. I would be welcome at the monastery but I had to know that there might be some setbacks as he was not well. Was I ready to travel long distances and risk not coming back with an interview for my television station?

Was I going to accept or pull back? I must confess that 'I grew slack from my first entrance in.' As is so often the case, pulling back would be easier. Taking no risks and let 'Love' take care of its own business. But as I read his books, it became clear to me that he was a figure of great importance. This wise monk spoke about the void inside and the inability to live up to standard models. But he also pointed to the path of transformation that Abbot Jeroen Witkam and Jef Boeckmans had opened up to me in Zen at the Trappist Monastery of Zundert in the Netherlands. So, was I going to organize a camera team for Colorado? What finally pulled me over was Father Thomas's citation of Carmelite sister Ruth Burrows, whom I had interviewed the year before in a remote part of Norwich, United Kingdom, and whom he admired. Kindred souls, they seemed to be. Indeed, 'You can't go wrong in this life if you trust God', he wrote. So, I packed my bags to go to 'Old Snowmass', not knowing what there was to come but accepting to be led by something which was greater than me.

> 'A guest,' I answered, 'worthy to be here':
> Love said, 'You shall be he.'
> 'I, the unkind, ungrateful? Ah, my dear,
> I cannot look on thee.'

I was told that the monastery would be tucked away in the Roaring Fork Valley of the Rocky Mountains. It was spring-time and on our way to the 'magic monastery'[11] we stopped to film the clouds gathering over Mount Sopris, the almost 13,000-foot mighty mountain. We recorded the sounds of the rushing water of the Roaring Fork River, as the snows had started to melt. The river had welled up near the ski resort Aspen, famous for its jet set on their glittering skis in their fancy outfits, not so far away from the monastery. I wondered if the rich and famous had ever heard of prayer, let alone Centering Prayer. But maybe they had! I remembered reading the story of the monk Bernie and his teasing remarks about the people of Aspen and the monks of the monastery.[12]

We followed the Roaring Fork River for a while on its way towards the Colorado River. What a long way the water had travelled to find its destiny. Had we done the same? What stories this river could tell, as monk Theophane had done in his beautiful little book.[13]

We were eager to get to our destination now. We stopped in the small hamlet called Woody Creek, got a few drinks and sandwiches, passed through Old Snowmass and drove into the Capitol Creek Valley. Finally, we entered the monastery proper, full of expectations.

> Love took my hand, and smiling did reply,
> 'Who made the eyes but I?'

I vividly remember seeing Father Thomas Keating for the first time in the flesh. He stood at the end of the long corridor of the monastery; a tall monk, stern, impressive yet gentle, looking inquisitively at our cameras, the film director, the camera men and finally at me. And then what I had feared most happened: he was not well and wanted to postpone the interview. My heart sank. We had travelled day and night to meet this monk. I had been aware of the risks, of course, so I started nervously to calculate the possibilities of this mission ever succeeding: my expensive camera team would leave in just three days. Would he be well soon? What was I to do?

For the moment, I was saved by the helpful abbot of the monastery, Father Joseph Boyle, who agreed to act as a replacement. Quite unexpectedly, this modest man proved to be a hidden gem that had lain undiscovered in the mountains. I sensed a spiritual life in him which he was rather unwilling to uncover for a camera at first. Yet, as our conversation grew more intense, he hinted towards the realm of silence he sometimes felt himself transported to. It was clear that there was an ongoing deepening in him that spoke louder than words. He invited us to vespers in the church of Mary. When the white monks stood in a circle, making a full profound bow, I was overwhelmed by the mystery of that moment. In the scarcely lit church, they softly but intensely prayed: 'Glory be to the Father and to the Son and to the Holy Spirit, as it was in the beginning, is now, and ever shall be, *World Without End*, Amen.' This was indeed a world without end, a spiritual realm in which Love could abide. But was it as beautiful as it appeared to be? Surely, there must be conflicts. I decided to ask Father Thomas, hoping that he would be better by the next day.

> 'Truth, Lord; but I have marred them; let my shame
> Go where it doth deserve.'
> 'And know you not,' says Love, 'who bore the blame?'
> 'My dear, then I will serve.'

Truth, I have often felt my eyes being marred. Deep feelings of insecurity, failure and emptiness have often invaded me. Father Thomas gently points out that I needn't worry too much and, most of all, I must not despair, which is the major temptation. Of course, he says, the spiritual journey is a long one and you can be overwhelmed by doubt. But self-criticism only strengthens the ego.

We can be saved by silence, by symbols and rituals. We may have to get a bulldozer to flatten the field when we start the transforming process that Centering Prayer is teaching. But we can give any name to God. Let's not be shy in naming Him, Father Thomas says. So much is waiting for us in the course of this journey. Don't be discouraged, 'God is prepared to give us millions of chances.' He even takes the blame upon himself: 'Word made flesh.'[14] So, yes, Father Thomas had indeed recovered enough to do the interview the next day and I was grateful for that. But then he astonished me even more when he was willing to describe an 'awakening' experience that had happened to him while being an abbot in Spencer. This most intimate of all experiences is hard to put into language, but he drew words and phrases out of his memory to make it vivid on camera. I admired him for considering this 'awakening' not as his own, but rather as given to him so that it could be shared by all.

Who knows where the end will be? Is there going to be an end? 'No,' Father Thomas says 'your consciousness can keep on growing, growing, growing.' Happiness is on your way, and so is suffering. Surely, death does not put an end to the journey, because 'once you have been born into this world, you never die'. Father Thomas himself, he tells me, has got the feeling that his spiritual journey is just beginning.

Going back to him a last time for yet another conversation, I felt like going to one of the renowned Desert Fathers of the fourth century – although a mountain father would be more appropriate here – to ask him the age-old pilgrim question: 'Abba, give me a word, how can I be saved?'

As my team is about to hit the road again, I rise at dawn to go a last time to the magic monastery, covered in the early-morning mist in a valley full of sounds of howling coyotes and roaring cattle. I cannot help but being overwhelmed by the dramatic scenery which is unfolding before me: the proud Rockies clad in the bright red light of the rising sun, the snow still on their peaks and deer sniffing at the windows of my lodge. I catch myself repeating the words of the abbot. 'Wow! Father, this is something!' But surely, it is not meant for me, *the unkind, the ungrateful*, as I notice George Herbert's words coming up in my mind. Why, though, should I doubt? Hasn't God proven to be greater than my thoughts, my imagination and my dreams at the end of this momentous journey? Am I not ready, finally, to serve?

As I reach the monastery and go in for Eucharist, I realize that I am late because I have been gazing too much at the wonderful scenery while being invaded by the transcendent. So, I am not at fault. The powerful though gentle One had put on a show for me. When I sit down on the hard benches of the church, being gazed on benevolently by a most beautiful Mary with child, I am just in time for Communion and I almost hear the abbot echoing George Herbert's words:

> 'You must sit down,' says Love, 'and taste my meat.'
> So I did sit and eat.

PART TWO

'To enter into the unveiled presence of God': conversations with Father Thomas Keating

A Lonely Time

> Let us take a minute of silence
> to open our hearts to the mystery of
> the divine indwelling within us

The longing for the sacred was already present in Thomas when he was a child. His early sensitivity would lead the young boy to sneak out of the family's comfortable apartment in New York to go to early Mass, without anybody knowing, without being able to talk about his yearnings with anyone.

This awareness deepened as he became a freshman at Yale University. He stopped attending social events as he had found something far more interesting. Instead of the club he was drawn to the chapel; instead of attending the lessons he was absorbed in books about the Christian mystics.

His family expected him to become a lawyer but he became a monk and a theologian instead, developing internationally into one of the most renowned spiritual teachers but not without feeling lonely at times.

What attracted you towards prayer when you were young?
What attracted me to prayer at the time of my conversion was my desperate need for spiritual help. I didn't have

anyone to speak to, and my friends could not figure out what I was doing. I found all my direction in the first three years in reading and studying the well-known Christian mystics, especially St Teresa of Avila and St John of the Cross.

Were books your sole inspiration? Didn't you need some kind of spiritual director?

There was none I could find in the area I was living until the second year after my conversion. In the library of Yale University, I found the four volumes of the *Homilies of the Church Fathers*, commenting on the four Gospels line by line. It gave me the conviction that the Christian religion has an important contemplative or mystical dimension. The Church Fathers wrote from that dimension, and their theological reflections and explanation of the gospel seemed to emerge from personal experience of the Christian mysteries. St Augustine of Hippo and the Cappadocian Fathers of the East are prime examples. I found this perspective immensely attractive and started reading some of the later mystics like St Teresa of Avila and St John of the Cross, who describes his spiritual journey in *Dark Night of the Soul*. I loved the poetical approach to the Bible of St John of the Cross, especially his description of silence: 'The eternal Father spoke only one Word and He spoke it in an eternal silence and it is in silence that we hear it.'

You were raised as a Roman Catholic. Nevertheless you experienced a kind of conversion towards 'a deeper Catholicism' when you were a freshman at Yale University. What conversion are you referring to?

I have been through many conversions. The one that took place at Yale in my first year there was the result of questioning the Catholic faith that I had brought with me from early life.

At the time of my conversion, I was leading the usual worldly life that adolescents are prone to. At Yale, I was challenged by the modern philosophers that we had to read. The chief book that influenced me was Leo Tolstoy's book about the kingdom of God and the Beatitudes, entitled *The Kingdom of God is Within You*.[1] It alerted me to the fact that many people who think themselves Catholics are not really catholic; at least, they are not following the gospel model, which is essentially, as Pope Francis teaches, the religion of the poor.

The poor are not just those who have few resources of a material kind. There are also those who are spiritually poor and morally bankrupt. The spiritually poor are those who lack the greatest resource of all, which is the conviction of God's presence within them as a loving God, healing their emotional and mental wounds, and inviting them to share the divine life, light and love. This is where true happiness is.

> The spiritually poor are those
> who lack the conviction
> of God's presence within them
> as a loving God

Unfortunately, we are born into this world without this knowledge of God's interior presence. We have to survive in social environments that are less than ideal. We have to live with our own incompleteness. The way into the fullness of union with God that the Bible speaks of is through the experience and acceptance of our weakness. All people feel incomplete. We are all desperately searching for happiness but in the wrong places. Even religious people, instead of manifesting God, a lot of the time manifest their false selves.

2

The Spiritual Journey

THE VOID INSIDE

'In the middle of the journey of our life, I found myself in a dark wood because I had lost the straight way. It is a hard thing to speak about that wilderness, it was so savage, harsh and impenetrable.'[2] On his journey through the turmoil of hell and purgatory, the Italian poet Dante is fortunate to find a guide in Virgil, an ancient Roman fellow poet.

A guide and a map are desperately needed on journeys. During his abbacy at Spencer, Father Thomas was inspired by the call for renewal by the Second Vatican Council as he reflected on the waning mystical tradition in the Catholic Church. Young persons had started flocking to the East while the richness of the Christian West lay hidden under the dust of centuries. Father Thomas, together with Father William Meninger[3] and Father Basil Pennington, audaciously decided to reclaim the Christian contemplative tradition.[4]

They designed a road map called 'Centering Prayer'[5] to uncover the wounded nature of human beings and expose the claims of the false self so that it can be transformed into the True Self. As in Dante's allegorical poem, paradise comes finally into sight. Yes, there can be an end to our sense of incompleteness and emptiness!

Why should we embark on a difficult spiritual journey? Leading a life in which we love one another, care for our family, enjoy good food, wine and travelling, can be very fulfilling. Shouldn't that be enough?

These are great values. They can be stepping stones to a relationship with God, who invites us to share eternal happiness with Him. They can also be disappointing and frustrating. Friendship with God can begin in this life. It puts other values in perspective and frees us from over-attachment to them.

There are many ways someone can go wrong in this life. Often people end up with finding a void inside. Does Centering Prayer, a method that you developed, make someone aware of the emptiness inside and the need to re-orientate oneself?

Centering Prayer as a path to contemplation is designed to heal the wounds of a lifetime. These wounds are brought about when we over-identify with our infantile emotional programmes for happiness. St Paul calls this condition 'the old man'. In either case, it is the result of coming into the world with the feeling of being separate from God, and seeking happiness in the passing pleasures of our instinctual life and in their gratification.

Self-consciousness begins to develop in very early childhood. An infant needs to feel loved, to feel a deep sense of security, the possibility of controlling its immediate situation and the gratification of its desires, all of which it mistakes for happiness.

Destroying the illusion

These emotional programmes for happiness arise from the illusion that we are separate from God; in other words, the false self, building on the separate-self sense, takes over our developing consciousness.

What is the false self?

The false self is born out of the exercise of the three emotional programmes for happiness: security and survival, affection and esteem, and power and control. A child needs each of those basic human needs to be provided for in some degree in order to survive.

There is no way of moderating these emotional programmes through reasoning since the child does not yet have the use of reason. These programmes easily become exaggerated, especially if they are withheld either by parents who were not good at the job or by the society in which the child lives. To further complicate the process, pre-packaged ideas and values are poured into a child by its teachers, its social milieu and environment, and even by its religion.

As a result of the frustration of its desires, a child exaggerates its basic need for security and survival, affection and esteem, and power and control, because they bring it satisfaction and gratification. For example: some people as they grow up become control freaks. Controlling other people is their chief satisfaction and pleasure! And it can become a demand in later life that we expect other people to respect.

What is the connection with religion?

What the religions are trying to do is to alert us to the fact that those instinctive desires are opposed to true happiness. Their excessive gratification will not bring anything but human misery. Something has to be done to heal those wounds. As I said, if they are extremely deep, the child seeks the gratification they may give with greater urgency. For example: security needs can then become a preoccupation. Affection and esteem needs can become an insatiable desire for praise, being loved by everybody, or the firm belief that 'no one should ever criticize me'. Power and control needs develop later, but you may notice these tendencies in a child very early in life. The need may even turn into the desire to control God! And this is not possible.

Do religions try to control God?

They can try to, because every human endeavour is shot through with the consequences of the emotional programmes for happiness, rooted as they are in the separate-self sense. The primary purpose of religion is to help us move beyond the separate-self sense to union with God. The unconscious wounds caused by the emotional programmes for gratification can be healed by becoming aware of them and most of all by facing up to them.

Is Centering Prayer a way of healing these wounds?

It is one way. Centering Prayer is basically a preparation for contemplative prayer. And contemplative prayer, or deep meditation in the terminology of the Eastern religions, is manifested in all the religious traditions in one way or another. They use different terminology which draws on the philosophies of their respective cultures, in order to express their teaching in language that can be understood by their contemporaries. Centering Prayer introduces us to interior silence, to the divine presence within us. It also helps us to face the dark side of our personality. Any form of deep meditation is designed for the same purpose. All religions recognize the sense of incompleteness in humans, but give different explanations for it.

Original sin is one explanation for why we feel incomplete. The science of biological evolution teaches that the problems of the human family are due to the fact that we are still evolving. Humans have evolved from their animal ancestry into the capacity for self-reflection, for developing abstract ideas like compassion and forgiveness, and for maturing into individual and social persons. The present level of creativity of our evolving rational consciousness has led to the extraordinary development of technology in our age.

> All religions recognize
> the sense of
> incompleteness in humans

Is the false self the same as the ego?

The ego is believed to be the full development of the false self. Others see the false self as the shadow side of the ego.

In any case, the ego is a necessary aspect that human beings need in order to grow up. During that process things can go wrong. For example, a child can be too withdrawn if it has not been allowed opportunities to experiment. So we make lots of mistakes. God doesn't approve of all that we do, but He knows we have to go through different kinds of situations in order to discover they don't work.

In meditative circles, it sometimes sounds as if the ego is the root of all evil. But can you do without it?
The ego must have a place: it develops and sustains our personality. One needs a strong ego in order to survive in this world. But eventually we have to let go of it.

Centering Prayer helps to heal the wounds of the human condition, the sense of incompleteness that Catholic Christians call original sin, which is one explanation for how we got into the human predicament. Other religions give other explanations but recognize the same problem. Teilhard de Chardin taught the theology of spiritual evolution. We have to let go of each stage of human development not by reacting against it, but by moving beyond it, integrating what was useful at every stage, but letting go of its limitations.

> Centering Prayer helps
> to heal the wounds
> of the human condition

We have probably all been wounded in our childhood. Nobody grows up without suffering. Do we all have to see a psychiatrist because we all need therapy?

If you live long enough, you begin to see that God is the master psychiatrist who practises a kind of divine therapy without our even asking. He knows us through and through and still loves us infinitely! Most people, of course, don't believe that. And that's the problem: they don't understand the goodness of God and His unlimited forgiveness and compassion. In the beginning of the spiritual journey, we don't know how to relate to God, so we invoke Him with our lips. After a while we begin to think of what we are saying. It gets serious when we experience God as father, mother, friend, brother, sister, beloved and spouse!

> Most people don't believe
> they are infinitely loved

Above all, we realize what a marvellous psychologist God is! He knows everything that is wrong with us. He knows all our secret and self-centred motivations and lovingly begins to show them to us according to our capacity at the present time.

Our developing and unfolding lives parallel the natural development of the universe and of human beings in general. God adjusts Himself to whatever amount of His reality we can accept at any particular point. In addition, there is a whole new cosmology evolving with the scientific discoveries of our time. Teilhard de Chardin was able to bridge the gap between religion and science in this area.

> How much of God's
> reality can you accept
> at this point?

What does it mean to be born in a state of woundedness?
Humanity has not yet evolved into fully human consciousness. We all suffer from the lack of personal evolution. We are born in a state of woundedness, but require rational consciousness in order to be capable of free choices. We are born without self-consciousness and with at least three absolute needs for security, love and control. If these are withheld as we saw, they tend to become exaggerated, and this is where our woundedness begins. We are moved instinctually to seek the gratification of these needs or to escape from the pain of their frustration. Every child seems to recapitulate the history of the human race from the predominance of instinctual animal needs through various levels of socialization, to full rational consciousness.

Given this state of woundedness, are we responsible for our actions?
This depends on our genuine capacity to make free choices. Psychology has raised the question as to what responsibility we have in the light of the discovery of the unconscious and the traumas many people are subjected to in early life. These wounds limit responsibility, depending more or less on their seriousness. For example: if we withhold the basic needs of an infant for security and love, and fail to meet its immediate discomfort, fears and lack of control, it can lead to its immense frustration. This hinders the forming of relations with its siblings and companions as life advances. Other disabilities, like mental illness, physical injury, early loss of parents, violence in the home, over-strictness or excessive permissiveness, can all reduce freedom of choice, and consequently reduce responsibility.

TRANSFORMATION

How can the false self be transformed into the true self?

The best way to do this is to let the false self die! It has no future. It is an obstacle to the experience of interior silence. Profound peace can then pervade one's whole being and remain even in the midst of immense difficulties and suffering.

> Profound peace can pervade one's whole life

How can this happen concretely?

Centering Prayer is based on the wisdom saying of Jesus in the Sermon on the Mount (Mt. 6:6) : 'If you want to pray, enter your inner room, close the door and pray to your Father in secret, and your Father who sees in secret will reward you.' Notice that 'Father' refers to a personal relationship, whether you call it father, mother, brother, soul-friend, spouse or anything else.

The first step in Centering Prayer is to enter your inner room, which is symbolized by the heart in most traditions; that is, your innermost self beyond the senses and beyond thinking. Choose a place that is fairly silent, where the phone doesn't ring, people don't talk to you, and the noise in the street is minimal.

Second, 'close the door', symbolizing your intention of letting go of all thoughts, preoccupations, memories and plans during this time. As soon as you are overtaken by thoughts, which is inevitable in the beginning, return to your original

Ask God to awaken what has been given to you

intention to let go of all thinking. You can do this in a very simple and extremely gentle way, like saying a sacred word briefly, noticing your breath, or turning to God with a brief glance of faith in His presence.

Finally, you pray in secret to the Father who speaks to you beyond words and who invites you to ever deeper silence.

In what way do these steps lead someone into interior silence or establish a deep relationship with the Father?
The steps that I have just mentioned are guidelines. Instead of using a word or noticing your breath, you can also use a sacred image to return to. These symbols do not *establish* you in interior silence; they simply reaffirm your original *intention* to be in God's presence and to be open to the divine action. The relationship develops in what might be called 'the office of the Divine Therapist', which is a metaphor for the inner room that Jesus speaks of. Centering Prayer as a way to interior silence is enhanced by practices that bring its fruits into daily life. The

fruit of this prayer is not something you produce. You simply reduce the obstacles by providing an interior environment in which the Spirit can speak without words in the inmost depths of your being.

As you practise Centering Prayer, you begin to experience the value of interior silence, which reveals the true self. The presence of God can also be experienced through the love of nature, deep friendship, conjugal love, generous service of others, or the discoveries of genuine science. There are many roads leading to the awakening of the original endowment that God has given every human being, of which the gift of contemplation is one. Contemplation has always been perceived as a gift in the Christian tradition, but it is a gift that has already *been given*. You have got it! What you have to do is to allow it to awaken within you. If God is absent, then all the wonderful things that people say about Him are absent too. Human nature is very fragile, and we will never understand ourselves or who we really are without the help of other people and especially the help of God.

> A gift
> that has already been given

Is it an innate capacity?

It is an innate part of human nature along with rational consciousness. Rational consciousness is, of course, an enormous leap forward in the development of consciousness from that of animal creatures. Animals follow their instincts while humans enjoy a measure of freedom of choice. Human development moves from almost nothing in the way of self-consciousness on the day of our birth, to ascending levels that evolve through experience, interaction with others and the wisdom teaching of spiritual traditions.

Are methods important?

Methods are prudent ways of going about things. Most of the world religions have methods that are very well thought out and which have been experienced by generations of practitioners. Zen, for instance, begins where reason leaves off. Of course, we must first have rationality before we can move beyond it.

As you begin the process of experiencing interior silence, you cultivate the growth of the relationship with God within you. This is done by periods of prayer in which you deliberately leave aside your thoughts, as we saw. Evagrius,[6] one of the early monastic fathers, said 'prayer is the laying aside of thinking'. That is a complete puzzle for people who are still dominated by their animal instincts and their emotional programmes of happiness.

People sometimes get upset if they can't control their thoughts during prayer. Do you have any advice for them?

When you get distracted in prayer, you may notice a certain heaviness of heart that may cause a feeling of separation from God. This happens in daily life as well. In both situations, you seem to be forgetting God, which is painful for someone who is seeking to remain in His presence in daily life. Examples: you see that you are over-absorbed in conversation or stuck on the video you are watching on your computer or reading too many things like the news of the day.

The presence of God that we seek in Centering Prayer and in daily life is not on the level of feelings. We can have unwanted thoughts and be preoccupied with things we have to do or want to do, while our deeper self is with God on the level of spiritual attentiveness, which is the abiding intention and desire to be always in God's loving presence.

Let go of the feeling of separation from God with its accompanying heaviness of heart. Then you can relax into the simple conviction of God's presence, while peacefully applying your mind to the action at hand.

Why can painful memories about the past arise during meditation?

Painful memories and emotions arise because in the course of Centering Prayer the defence mechanisms that have hidden our deep psychological wounds and dark traumas from early childhood are released, and the emotional wounds of early childhood come to consciousness. Humility and trust in God help us to face the humiliations of the false self as self-knowledge increases with the practice of prayer.

Centering Prayer heals the unconscious by allowing the repressed material from early childhood that is secretly influencing our decisions, motives and relationships to come to consciousness so that we can acknowledge them and then let them go. Normally, as soon as you perceive them, you want to get rid of them. This can be an 'aha' moment. Some, however, are so well hidden that you may need professional help. But such help can only go so far. The dark nights described by St John of the Cross reach more deeply into our unconscious.

Is meditation, which seems rather passive, necessary in order to be a Christian? What about people with active temperaments?

Meditation is certainly a great help for people in order to be Christians, especially if they want to grow in the dispositions of love of God and neighbour. Active temperaments are just as capable of this as anyone else. In any case, meditation is one of the best *activities* there is.

What symbols are dear to you in this transformative process?
Symbols are valuable when they speak to you of where you are in your spiritual development. For me the Eucharist is a tremendous symbol as well as an amazing reality. In Holy Communion we are thrust into the furnace of divine love and into the bosom of the Trinity. You begin to feel comfortable with the mystery that the symbol is pointing to. The spiritual life is fundamentally an experience that presupposes human reason, but it also includes the spiritual capacities of your inmost self. Through spiritual practices, these are gradually put together.

The cloud is another symbol of spiritual development. It is used by the anonymous author of the fourteenth-century manuscript, *The Cloud of Unknowing*, a book that Father William Meninger discovered in some forgotten corner of the monastic library. As a manual on how to do contemplative meditation, it is basic to the method of Centering Prayer. What does it say about thoughts during prayer?
This book is a masterpiece. It strongly recommends putting all your thoughts during prayer into the 'cloud of forgetting'. At the same time it urges you to keep knocking on the Cloud of Unknowing through frequent turning to God in pure faith. Difficulties tend to intensify our desire for God. As our confidence in God increases, the realization of how unworthy of God we are arises in our awareness, not as a

34

pathology as in people who are self-hating, but because that is the truth.

We are creatures and we have to acknowledge our creaturehood in order for God to take over our lives completely. Even when we acknowledge our unworthiness, it normally takes time for us to agree to its full implications. At the same time we must continue to trust in God's infinite mercy.

Another mystic you admire for her insights that brought about a major renewal of contemplative prayer in the Catholic Church is St Thérèse of Lisieux.[7] What makes her so special?

Thérèse taught that God is a loving father, partly perhaps because she had a very loving biological father. Both of her parents were canonized in December 2015. She had a special insight into the way God treats people. In the case of some, she says, He sees the dangers in their path and removes all the obstacles in advance. For others, He allows them to fall into sin and then lovingly forgives them. That's a wonderful insight! You can't go wrong in this life if you trust God. It doesn't matter what you have done. God is eager not only to forgive you, but to give you everything He can give that you are willing to receive. He even makes amends to the people you may have injured.

PERILS AND OPPORTUNITIES

Doubt

Didn't you ever doubt?

Sure, but you can get over that. You have to *decide* to trust God. Doubt is an important quality of human nature because most of our ideas about God need to be doubted.

The purification that the divine psychotherapy offers helps us to realize that our ideas of God are inadequate. We tend to think of Him only in terms of the senses and rational consciousness. But He transcends infinitely whatever concepts we have of Him. He intends to raise us to a divine perspective similar to His own, so that He can give Himself to us and bring us into His own boundless beatitude.

> Even our idea of God
> is a mistake

Are you referring to the 'negative theology'[8] in Christianity: you cannot define God because He transcends any definition?
Exactly. The night of the spirit, which is the most intense level of the divine therapy, frees you from the domination of your emotional programmes for happiness. At the same time it frees you from limited ideas about God so that you can accept God as the Unknowable. He remains lovable at every stage. Divine love comes to us through the deepening of interior silence in prayer and the reduction of our selfish programmes for happiness. A big project!

You have started one!
No one can start such a project except God. Even disasters have a loving divine purpose that eventually will appear. I think it was a masterpiece of divine wisdom to start human nature off with the experience of its extreme weakness and ignorance. Otherwise, we would all come to be as proud as Lucifer.

The night of the Spirit frees you from your limited ideas about God

How do you deal with doubt? Can it ever have positive consequences?

If you can sit through the problems that arise in prayer, such as doubts or confusion, you may be pushed to a higher level of consciousness where you perceive that what you thought were opposites are actually complementary and become one in the higher stages of consciousness. Then apparent opposites are synthesized.

> Religion
> is not an end in itself

To see a problem such as boredom or a sense of absence as an invitation to a higher stage of consciousness and creativity is better than trying to get rid of it. Trying to get rid of it, including the suffering involved, is not the right approach. You have to accept what is happening as God's loving action. That requires some way of getting acquainted with who God is. That is actually what religion is for. It is not an end in itself, but a means of giving us a conceptual background and a discipline of ritual, prayer and symbols that enable us to open more and more to self-surrender, trust in God and humility.

> A problem is an invitation
> to a higher stage of consciousness

But aren't mercy and justice opposites of one another?
The inevitable opposites belonging to rational consciousness, such as justice and mercy, are often impossible to reconcile on the rational level, but are resolved when that level is transcended. On these higher levels of consciousness diversity is enriching rather than separating.

OBSTACLES

What obstacles can arise from the point of view of the aspirant? How can they be overcome?
Many values from the culture in which we were brought up are accepted unquestioningly, but are not necessarily religious values. A common one is 'you should always succeed'. To be a high achiever is the major goal of American education. But whether it is acknowledged or not, it can never work. You can never be a high-enough achiever to satisfy the pride that wants to be on top of every profession, occupation,

and to be esteemed by everybody. These are still infantile attitudes that hinder the path to true freedom and enduring happiness.

Deep meditation and contemplative prayer are central to ridding ourselves of the obstacles of selfishness, which are indifference to other people's needs, over-identification with our culture or group, attachment to prestige and wealth, and the seeking of compensatory sense pleasures in food, drink and sexual activity.

What's the problem with sexuality?

Sexuality in conjugal love is a great gift of God. It brings the experience of God to many people, but is easily abused when it is engaged just to give oneself pleasure. In the Christian idea of marriage it is meant to be a gift and a service. Married persons serve each other's sexual needs. Procreation is of course essential for the whole evolutionary process of the human race. Relationship with God does not deny that truth, but discovers that we need to integrate all our experiences into an ever more profound relationship with God.

You mentioned that sexuality can be easily abused. What's the nature of sexuality?

Sexuality is a very powerful energy and necessary for most humans to enable them to express their generativity in some way. Even in a celibate lifestyle, sexuality has to be expressed somehow, and this can be done through generous acts of service, such as ministry, spiritual direction and the works of mercy.

Sexuality is just energy, so it's how we use it that is important. To deny it completely does not seem to be the proper way to integrate it for most people.

> Sexuality is a very powerful energy
> but easily abused

Everything in human experience comes in a package that is never quite perfect. Creation is essentially incomplete, but we have been called to share the divine life itself. This requires faith. God is the most wonderful presence; it just *is*, without any qualification. As long as this presence is broken down into particular experiences, it is not yet God, because God is everything at the same time.

The interest in the spiritual journey seems to be growing in our hectic times. What obstacles arise from the point of view of the teacher?
There is a recent renewal of contemplative prayer throughout Christianity. Centering Prayer is one of the methods contributing in a modest way to this awakening.

The spiritual journey is not something we learn about all at once. The journey takes time. The present-day interest in spirituality is not necessarily rooted in a religion. What discipline is going to be used to train people in practices that are normally necessary to receive divine communications in an experiential way?

Another issue is how to reach young aspirants at a deep level. Many young people read nothing except what is on the internet and then reply immediately. There is little time for reflection. The capacity to relate to others is necessary to relate to God, who might be defined as Relationship itself. God is present to everything and to everyone and is prepared to give Himself to us if only we are willing to consent.

Are there other ways as well to embark on this journey?

Centering Prayer is one of the methods to awaken the contemplative dimension in one's life. There are other methods that are very good too, like the World Community for Christian Meditation that Father Laurence Freeman, OSB, has spread all over the world. He has started a meditation centre on campus at Georgetown University, Washington, DC, which attracts students from other religious traditions. Father Richard Rohr has created a wisdom school that has many aspirants. People go twice a year to his Center for Action and Contemplation in Albuquerque, New Mexico, to interact with others for a week and listen to talks given by experts. The two-year course itself is online.

Since most people can't travel because of the expense, they could form small groups where they live, learn the basics, share their journeys with each other, and read the literature recommended by various wisdom teachers.

In Centering Prayer, the teacher can be anyone who is well experienced and committed to the transformative process and who has an appreciation of how rewarding and at the same time how difficult this journey is. The journey, as time goes on, requires letting go of everything to which we are overly attached.

If you have to let go of the things you love, do you have to lead an ascetic life as a Christian?

Notice I said *overly* attached. Few can leave everything at once to follow a traditional path to contemplation. But everyone has to deal with the human condition, which is one of woundedness, and needs some healing of mind and body to prepare for contemplation. Only the love of God, growing in us through prayer, meditation and the service of others, can enable us to let go of the things we love, whether these are good, bad or in between.

A NEW MONASTICISM

What role do you as a monk and a spiritual teacher see for the monastery in this journey? Could lay people rely on it without having to become a monk or a nun?

There is a movement today called the *new monasticism*. The idea is to practise monastic values while living in the world, without a commitment to a specific religious order and which is open to the wisdom of other world religions. This is admirable and challenging, especially for people who are serious seekers of God. But, as I mentioned before, the problem still remains: where and how are they going to be trained, and in what discipline? The movement of contemporary spirituality contains people who are from different religious backgrounds and from no religion. Can they agree on a basic method and receive the kind of training needed to reduce the obstacles to contemplation? The monastery is a place where there is a stable population of people who can offer good advice in order to help aspirants grow in the practice of contemplative prayer. Without that kind of discipline, I don't think that contemplation can be fully appreciated, practised or become transforming.

Could Christianity disappear? What opportunities do you see to invigorate it?

I don't think Christianity will disappear, but it may have fewer people involved in it. It needs to provide opportunities for contemplative living in the world out of its rich mystical tradition. For instance: a monastic environment where young people could go for a time and learn about contemplative prayer.

What do you think about the criticism that monastic life withdraws from the world in order to do nothing?

Withdrawing from the world by letting go of our significant attachments is a means to see what its basic values are, so that God, like a scientist in a laboratory, can see what we will do in various kinds of situations and difficulties. The spiritual journey has dark nights that enable us to unite with Christ in his experience on the cross and his descent into hell. Hell is a state of consciousness more than a place. God, as scripture affirms, wants everyone to be saved. He knows how to bring that about since He is infinitely creative.

Right now, the personal challenge we are experiencing is one of many possibilities, and one that God must think is best for us. 'Everything just as it is, is perfect', according to Zen Buddhist teaching. The perfection may include our willingness or determination to help everyone in need and to lay down our life for the transformation of the human family into union and oneness with God.

Nevertheless, monks are often reproached for living a passive life and not engaging in charity, for instance. What do you think about this criticism?

That could happen. It's not certain what exact form monastic life will take in the twenty-first century. It was a life close to the soil in past centuries. The ancient monks earned their living from working on the land. Now, they have been industrialized like everyone else, and most monasteries have to have an industry to survive. Will there be problems for monks who no longer do manual labour in the fields or have the sense of being close to nature, but spend all day looking at their computers? Monastic prayer alone will not bring about the transformation that they are seeking.

Everything, including monastic life, is changing. All the religions have to be up to date in a world in which science has become the primary authority for almost everything. Unfortunately, science is very limited in moral and spiritual perception. Religion and science need to support each other. For example, dialogue between science and religion is important in our time in order to increase the vision of God as the Creator of all. Many religious leaders do not have the contemplative experience to see, as Pope Francis does, that mercy is the name of the game. It is not possible to be merciful unless you realize that you have received gratuitously the infinite love and mercy of God.

> Mercy is the name of the game

Isn't it difficult for ordinary people who have got a job, a mortgage and things to do, to practise Centering Prayer and to develop it, like you, a monk in a monastery, have been able to?
It is just as hard in a monastery and harder in some ways. At least, outside in the world, you have various distractions, other people to interact with, and lots of things to do. Reducing your preoccupations gives God a chance to concentrate on your growing relationship with Him. Interior silence is the best way to access our innermost self where God dwells. That's why periods of silence deserve to be put high on everyone's list of occupations.

3

Close Encounters

Father Thomas can occasionally hear the hum of a bulldozer, as St Benedict's Monastery houses a ranch as well. The horses' stable is overlooked by a statue of a small white Madonna watching from afar over her little mountain community of about a dozen monks. Closer to the monks, in the sober monastery church where the stones are imbued with monks' prayers, a huge stained-glass window in bright coloured glass portrays her in full stature. As the first rays of sunlight hit her image at dawn, it lights up as if it were on fire, and the 'Glory to the Father, the Son and the Holy Spirit' becomes visible in the form of a woman. This is a World without End. For centuries, monks have praised Our Lady and will continue to do so, even if they are killed like the Trappist monks of Thiberine, Algeria.

What happens if God and man come close? Father Thomas realized that the goal in a monastery was not austerity but 'coming close'. Outside the monastery, he saw people frantically looking for happiness while experiencing God as absent. The teacher, which he had become, encouraged people to be transformed and to undertake drastic changes. Get a bulldozer! Make smooth the path, dive into the deep waters of stillness and silence which seem to precede the awakening. One thing is for sure: we'll be surprised by God who escapes all our naming and our efforts to define Him.

THE ILLUSION

Many people have got the idea that God is absent or even non-existent. You call this a monumental illusion. Why?
Because God is really all there is! God is so present that nothing else is present by comparison. We are manifesting God even in the worst things that we do. God is everywhere and there cannot be any reality without Him. Our idea of God from early religious education has to be enlarged. Religion is a stepping stone to awakening to an intimate relationship with God. With practice you can become completely identified with the divine presence and detached from your own ego. Even self-consciousness begins to diminish because you are becoming more concerned about God and His concerns rather than your own. We won't get to this place by meditation alone. To know who we really are requires a community, people whose behaviour tests the genuineness and sincerity of our formal prayer.

What is needed then?
The great question is: who are you? It is certainly not your resumé, not your personality, nor even your true self. The true self in the Christian tradition is the image of God in us manifesting through the fruits and gifts of the Spirit.

God speaks to us in silence. Some people say they have heard God speak in words, but the message is always filtered through their culture, education or religious convictions. They have to realize that, even if God speaks to them, it is a very limited form of communication and they can misunderstand it. There is a much deeper communication waiting for us as the result of deep interior silence.

> God speaks in silence,
> He doesn't usually use words

Prayer in secret (Mt. 6:6) is the result of interior silence becoming stillness. Then there is not only no movement by way of thoughts, but no movement at all. That's why people who are deep meditators hardly move. Prayer in secret also heals the hatred of self that may develop because of guilt feelings or the negative effects of oppression and repression. To achieve its full effect, prayer in secret has to be assisted by practices that bring its insights and peace into daily life, so that daily life becomes a contemplative practice in the midst of activity.

Is praying a sign of a developed stage of a human being?
Yes, if you mean by 'praying', having a relationship with God. This can go on developing in intensity and in intimacy all one's life.

Is it an illusion to see action and contemplation as two separate things? Are they basically one, as the mystics say?
At some point in the transformative process, you never lose sight of the presence of the divine Beloved, even in the midst of activity. After all, God is always at rest and always in action, and we have to learn to be the same. Those who are completely united to God are always in God's presence. They are praying unceasingly or, more exactly, the Spirit is praying in them.

To allow this stage of consciousness to take over our life, we need to let go of preconceived ideas and the unquestioned assumptions of our education and culture. If you don't do what the culture thinks is important, you are likely to be ostracized. People who are not on the spiritual journey tend to persecute those who are, or avoid them because they do not know what to say to them. They are looking for happiness in the possession and gratification of worldly goods, whereas happiness can only be found on a transcendent level of consciousness where body, mind and spirit are united in total surrender to God.

You previously mentioned that God can adjust to every level of consciousness. Is He so close to us that He adjusts to each one of us?
The development of consciousness parallels the development of human beings in general. It evolves from zero self-consciousness in infancy to a conscious relationship with loving parents. It later develops a capacity for broader and deeper relationships during adolescence. Then it settles into full responsibility for itself and its choices, which is the sign of adulthood. Adulthood brings maturity, and finally the dying process. Illnesses are loving warnings from God that we can't stay forever in this life. To bring the insights and perspectives of adult consciousness into daily life challenges us to love other people genuinely, including our enemies. God is infinite so He is everywhere at once and is doing everything at once. He is completely present to us where we are and nudges us to take the next step in the development of consciousness. For Christians, growth of consciousness is growth in faith, hope and love.

> Illnesses are loving warnings from God
> that we can't stay forever in this life

NAMING THE DIVINE

Who should we call 'good'?

'Only God is good' according to Jesus. The goodness we see in others is not theirs but God working in them, trying to help them to integrate their animal instincts into the rational powers of a human being, and then to transcend them. These rational powers are a great contribution to the human race, but there is more to the journey than that. Giving yourself completely to God as an instrument or as a channel of His goodness and love is to co-redeem the world with Christ.

In our conversations, you have used the name 'divine indwelling' to indicate God. What does it mean?

It means that God is present within us all the time as the source of our being at every level. He is present beyond thinking. You cannot contain God in some mental container. By

A presence beyond thinking

becoming aware of your incapacity to do anything without God, you turn yourself over completely to the transformative process in which God awakens within you, so to speak, as your deepest and inmost self.

Do you give a name to God?

Give Him any name you like. Actually, 'God' isn't the best word because it is so misused. The term means something different for almost everybody. In an inter-spiritual dialogue group that I participated in, we discussed this question at great length. We realized that we must let go of our limited and limiting ideas and embrace the fact that God is bigger than any reality we know. We agreed on the name 'the Ultimate Reality'.

More important than the name we give to God is to realize that the relationship is both personal and transpersonal at the same time. God treats us with great wisdom, tenderness and care. He helps us to get free of our self-centred tendencies, as well as our ignorance, and to be open to every other human being, who also has the same invitation to a relationship of oneness with God.

> The feeling of self-hate
> is just another illusion of the false self

This insight creates compassion for other people and a greater willingness to see and acknowledge how weak we are. Your weakness is not an enemy, but a stepping stone to depend completely on God. These are the two basic steps in Alcoholics Anonymous. The first step is realizing that you are so helpless that your life has become unmanageable. The second step is to turn your life completely over to God, no matter how worthless you feel yourself to be. The feeling of self-hate is just another illusion of the false self, caused by pride based on the fact that you don't measure up to some standard imposed on you in childhood or by the culture in which you live. You are convinced that happiness can only be found in the gratification of your emotional programmes for happiness and acceptance by the group you identify with, which is sheer nonsense.

> Your weakness is not an enemy
> but a stepping stone

In adolescence you often become aware of how much of the advice you received in childhood isn't much help. In fact, some of your overly dependent relationships were damaging. The only self we know at that age is the false self. It is hard to let go of it unless you experience something better. Such is the experience of God's presence beyond the senses and thinking. You begin to realize that your whole being is sustained by the divine energy, a power greater than yourself. That energy is willing to take over our lives, to live in us, and to bring us through physical death into union with Ultimate Reality itself.

> It's very hard to let go of your false self
> unless you experience something better

What is this Ultimate Reality?

In Christianity we call this the Trinity: Father, Son and Holy Spirit. But some Eastern religions have another revelation;

they think of God as non-personal. Granted that He *is* non-personal, He is *also* personal at the same time. We should think of both as one and the same Reality and integrate the two so that these perceptions are not in opposition. That brings about a genuine respect for other people's belief systems, even though we do not agree with everything they believe in. In any case, we do not judge or condemn anyone and we respect their religious practices. The Holy Spirit dwells in them as well as in us.

In many cases we can learn from other traditions, including certain teachings that our tradition may have put on the back-burner. Every religion needs to be renewed and expanded as the experience of practitioners who are seeking God with the whole of their being becomes more widespread. For the Abrahamic traditions, everything is contained in the first commandment to love God with all your heart, with all your soul, with all your mind, and with all your strength. The second commandment is to love your neighbour as yourself. We are all in desperate need of being loved. To be loved is what brings people to life.

You mentioned that the Ultimate Reality in Christianity is called the Trinity: Father, Son and Holy Spirit. Is God one or three?

According to Christian doctrine, God is three persons in one divine nature. Some contemporary theologians prefer the term 'relationships' to 'persons'. The doctrine of the Trinity reveals the meaning of the universe, which is sacrifice: giving oneself away. This is the disposition of the Father, who empties His entire divine nature into the Son, who in turn returns all that he has received back to the Father in the unity of the Holy Spirit. This total giving away of all that each member of the Trinity possesses with regard to the divine nature constitutes the boundless joy of the Father and the Son. Their mutual and infinite love for each other is the Holy Spirit. They live in each other rather than in themselves. Thus sacrifice – the giving away of all that one is – is the meaning of the universe. In the Trinity, sacrifice is delightful. In the world of human beings it is bound to be painful.

Doctrine always sounds a bit abstract. Is it possible to give an example of the giving away of self and the 'emptying' you speak about?

The incarnation of the Second Person of the Trinity, whom scripture reveals as the Son of the Father and Source of all that is, is the classical manifestation of 'emptying'. The text of St Paul that describes this emptying is as follows: 'Be of the same mind as Christ Jesus, who though he is by nature God, did not consider his equality with God a condition to be clung to, but emptied himself by taking on the nature of a slave, fashioned as he was in the likeness of men and recognized in outward appearance as a man. He humbled himself and became obedient to death; yes, to death on a cross' (Phil. 2:5–8).

The Trinity is hardly ever mentioned in sermons nowadays. It seems as if the subject is carefully avoided. What could be the reason for that? Is it not central in Christianity?

It's the supreme revelation of the Christian religion from which all the other mysteries emerge. 'Mystery' in this context means that no rational explanation is possible. No theological reflections can do more than point to it. Although the knowledge of the Trinity cannot be known by human reason, love can penetrate the 'cloud of unknowing' and experience God's presence. There is a renewal in theology taking place today with regard to this central and deepest mystery of Christianity.

Bernard of Clairvaux, the most powerful propagator of Cistercian reform, writes that the Trinity is 'food for the more advanced' people on the spiritual level.[9] Would you agree with that? Or do you see ways to share this mystery with everybody without preconditions?

Like all the doctrines of the various religions, there are ascending insights or perspectives relating to advancing levels of faith and consciousness. Beginners along the path can't see the depth and spiritual richness of these teachings until their practice and experience of God matures. That seems to be what St Bernard has in mind by the term 'advanced'. The Trinity as the deepest and most profound of Christian doctrines is the prime example of the growth of spiritual understanding through purification of the false or self-made self and ego, into union and unity with that Mystery of Oneness.

'GET A BULLDOZER!'

It seems that stillness and silence are preconditions in order to continue our life's journey without falling back into old mistakes. What exactly is meant by stillness?

By letting go of all thought as a regular practice in Centering Prayer, interior silence is gradually enhanced like delicious perfume billowing through a particular space. Thoughts get fewer, and you may even experience moments of no movement of mind or body at all. This is called 'stillness'. It is the term that is used in the Psalms: 'Be still and you will know that I am God' (Ps. 46:10). That is exactly what Centering Prayer as a daily practice is doing. But you have to do it every day, preferably twice a day, rain or shine. We need the daily practice of a discipline of mind and body to get over the habits of a lifetime and our general lack of mental discipline.

With some people, ease in meditating does not come until about forty years of age, and with others it doesn't seem to come at all, but it's there, waiting to be awakened. In the Eastern religions, they call the full development, enlightenment. There are enlightened persons today but they are extremely rare. It normally takes a long time to experience the fruits that come from long-range perseverance in prayer and meditation. Such a discipline changes the structure of the brain and frees us over time from the emotional programmes for happiness. When the discipline has been practised for thirty or forty years, or even longer, new structures will be formed that are free of the domination of tyrannical habits of behaviour.

The brain translates all sense experiences into the habitual ways established early in life. The first step, you might say, is to get a bulldozer, remove the habitual pathways down which we send the energies of the brain, and flatten the playing field. Then you can build new channels in the brain that respond to true human values and the deeper values that the Spirit inspires.

The purpose of our historical lifetime is to provide us with the time and space for the integration and the transformation of body, soul and spirit. The infant is totally under the influence of its needs and emotional programmes designed to gratify them. The adolescent finds them even more complex because of the socialization period that begins around seven or eight. A strong commitment to the transforming process is the basic meaning of conversion. It is the determination to radically change the direction in which we are looking for happiness; that is, from self-centred projects to the unconditioned love of God.

What's the role of silence?

Silence is the language of God. All other divine communications can only be poor translations. Like any language, you have to learn it in order to understand what is being said. That requires becoming aware that one's habitual way of responding to daily life is rooted in selfish motivation from which we need to be liberated if we are to perceive the voice that speaks without words.

> Silence is the language of God;
> all the rest is a poor translation

The false self is an accumulation of inherited, emotional and infantile instinctual needs that have to be integrated in the course of growing up into rational consciousness and later into the wisdom of the great spiritual traditions. That's a big job.

The spiritual journey is a lifetime commitment. We would be overwhelmed if God showed us all our faults at once. Instead He gently and gradually instructs us. The language of God is not in words. He has sometimes allegedly spoken in words, as we previously observed, but words must pass through our rational apparatus, which is under the influence of the false self and its emotional programmes for happiness. We can misunderstand spiritual communications and experiences even when they are genuine.

He gently instructs us

Our many faults can be hidden from us, especially in a culture that accepts them and even encourages them. In America everybody wants to get rich quick. People think this is the road to happiness, whereas it is an almost certain formula for human misery.

Do we need rituals or can we simply discard them as belonging to some old form of religion?
Rituals, images and symbols are necessary for most people to get over their over-identification with the raw material of childhood and adolescence. Our five senses and our thinking apparatus can be stepping stones to a deeper knowledge of God. Nothing is ever rejected in our development, nor should we try to reject it. It is incorporated into the next step of our development if we continue the practice of Centering Prayer or other methods that lead to contemplation.

Nothing is ever rejected in our development

Can our motivation become lacking?
Motivation is extremely important. We must keep practising for the love of God, not to please ourselves. Contemplative development, at least in Centering Prayer, becomes interior stillness and moves into pure consciousness. It is then indistinguishable from the traditional contemplative life described by the great mystics of the Christian mystical tradition.

Contemplative life in the Christian tradition has the goal of transforming us in such a way that God lives in us more than we do. This gift to every person is a concrete sign of God's love. Suffering helps to see this truth, if we can accept it. When you love the wrong things, especially if you are attached or addicted to them, you are going to have problems. If you have been very damaged in early childhood, you can only be healed by being greatly loved by someone who puts love into your life, perhaps for the first time. It is hard to become fully human without the conviction and feeling of being loved.

> You can only be healed
> by being greatly loved

Becoming pure

4

Awakening

Father Thomas was sitting in the small round parlour at the west wing of the monastery; a window behind him offered a magnificent view of the Rocky Mountains. Their tops were covered in a light layer of snow but they were fully alive, in the way only mountains can be. Looking at these silent moments of creation, I was transported back to Mount Fuji in Japan where I had conversed with another spiritual giant, the Dominican friar and Zen teacher Vincent Shigeto Oshida.[10] He had stressed the necessity of becoming pure of heart. The sayings of this Eastern teacher, with Mount Fuji behind, seemed to find an echo in the words of the Western Father Thomas today. East and West intertwined.

I knew that Father Thomas was familiar with the Eastern spiritual traditions. I also knew he had been inspired by the writings of the Desert Fathers and Mothers of early Christianity, who used the term 'pure prayer' to indicate the ability to circumvent thought in order to rest directly in the presence of the divine. But could theory turn into reality? I was amazed by his answer.

Is awakening the last step in Centering Prayer?

Stillness in Centering Prayer gradually evolves into pure awareness, which is also called awakening. In contemplative stillness, you may have thoughts, but they are unwanted and you easily disregard them. This, though, takes time and the purification of the unconscious by the infused dark nights. I am talking about years. In pure consciousness there are no thoughts at all during the period of formal prayer. This becomes one's habitual experience. With this infused wisdom, the realization of our deep hunger for God grows. We experience the profound incompleteness in ourselves that is not fulfilled. We cry out from the bottom of our heart to God's healing power. The human condition at the present time is starving for God.

> The human condition at the present time
> is starving for God

What do we awaken to? Is this method designed for everybody?

We have to accept our unlikeness to God and submit to the divine therapy, which is more profound and liberating than psychoanalysis or psychotherapy.

We must draw on the skills of therapy to help people who have special problems like severe depression, schizophrenia and the post-traumatic stress syndrome that is afflicting so many veterans. The latter cannot practise silence easily because it opens them to memories that are unbearable. It brings to the surface guilt feelings from actions that were required of them by military authorities, but were against their cultural and moral convictions and conscience. They are persecuted by these negative and unbearable thoughts and memories. There is a form of meditation that uses the breath to ground the silence of meditation in the body so that they can forget the overwhelming memories of traumatic experiences which they cannot ordinarily control, and that psychological treatments or medication cannot normally help them with.

Can you tell us something about the experience you had when you were recovering from an operation at St Joseph's Abbey, Spencer, Massachusetts, where you were the abbot?

I have called this experience an *awakening*. It was not the kind of full and permanent enlightenment that some people have received after lengthy practice. Our friends in the East use the word enlightenment. The best word for it in English seems to be awakening, since many mystics teach that we already have the divine presence as an integral part of human nature, but are unaware of it.

Awakening to what?

To what is! You can prepare for it by reducing the obstacles that are the projects of the false self which look for happiness in the wrong places. Everybody makes mistakes because everybody is born *without* a sense of God's presence that would give us a standard to judge the true value of experience. That divine presence within us and how to reach it is the main focus of the spiritual journey.

What led you towards this experience?

I was conscientious in the practice of my religion and its rituals. Rituals in most religions are meant to bring us to a personal relationship with the Ultimate Reality. That Ultimate Reality, of its very nature, is in relationship with everything that exists, and this relationship is primarily one of love.

Can you put into language what happened on that day of your *awakening* in the Spencer monastery?

What happened on that occasion as I stepped outside the monastic infirmary, where I was recovering from a hernia operation, is that the Presence that we are seeking in Christian contemplation showed up in my consciousness without any introduction. *The experience was one of boundless love, mercy, forgiveness, tenderness, intimacy, patience and enormous affirmation and reassurance all at the same instant.* God until then was still just an idea, but God *as God is* was for a brief time an invisible Presence that pervaded my whole being and consciousness. I looked at a nearby tree, and my whole life was shown there in a few seconds. Then I was led into a hayfield where I perceived the divine energy emerging out of the ground in the form of endless creativity.

You also mentioned that your experience lasted for an hour or so and provoked a lot of joy. Was there no hint of God as a judge or someone to be afraid of, or was it only joy you experienced?

It was only joy and amazement. I even detected what seemed to be a slight amusement on God's part at my amazement in experiencing such intimacy. I couldn't believe it, and I couldn't deny it.

What was the essence of your experience?

It was *that I was loved by God* in a totally gratuitous way! We usually have negative ideas about ourselves, especially if we have high ideals and fail to measure up to them. If the spiritual journey is a long trip, it is because we don't know how to consent to God right away, but have to be edged gradually into realizing that we can't do any good entirely on our own.

We depend on God by giving ourselves completely to Him and by letting Him choose the situations arising each day of our lives. This means that we accept what happens. We do not attribute the good results to ourselves, but to the Spirit who urges us to express in practice the spiritual values and dispositions that we are receiving.

Has the experience stayed with you or has it faded with time? Has it changed your consciousness, your life?
It has certainly faded but it gave me a new understanding of God's goodness and a greater capacity to endure suffering, humiliation and difficulties of all kinds.

Does everybody receive the awakening or enlightenment in the course of the spiritual journey? How can the awakening manifest itself in everyday life?
Awakening as I described it earlier is the goal of the spiritual journey, a stage of human consciousness that some call unity consciousness or oneness. One's whole being is taken over by God so that the Holy Spirit inspires and guides all the actions of the subject of His grace. It can be hidden from others. It manifests itself in compassion for all creation, interior freedom, boundless confidence in God and His mercy, forgetfulness of self and permanent union with God. *It frees a person from suffering, but this person becomes vulnerable and open to sharing the sufferings of everyone else.* In other words, Christ's sufferings for the healing and transformation of the human family may be relived in us for the healing and salvation of humanity.

You just mentioned that our difficulties arise because we don't know how to consent to God right away. How can we consent? How to do it concretely?

Consent is the simplest deliberate action you can take in any situation. It requires little or no effort. It is just an *intention*, a 'yes', to whatever is happening.

In Centering Prayer we sit down in a quiet place and put ourselves in the presence of God. No word or gesture is really necessary. As long as we let the unwanted thoughts go by, there is nothing we need to do. The rest is up to God. The relationship is established by our original intention to spend this time in God's presence. When we notice ourselves engaging with thoughts that may arise, we ever-so-gently return to our breath or the sacred word we have chosen as the symbol of our intention to consent to God's presence and action.

You have had a deep transforming experience. As a consequence, you may be better qualified to see what is lacking in this world.

Intimacy with God is what is missing in this world, even in the world religions. Realizing how much God loves every man and woman emerges over a period of time in contemplative prayer. This prayer itself evolves into more and more profound experiences until you realize that the greatest experience of God is no experience or rather, God is *beyond* all experience. We must relate to God on God's terms. Then we will know that the created universe, our religion, and everything else are stepping stones towards learning that God is beyond the experiences of the senses and thinking. The external senses are transformed into spiritual senses in the process; that is, they reveal various ways in which God is continuously relating to us.

The bottom line is that love alone counts: not sentimental love, not co-dependency, not selfish love in the sense of 'What am I going to get out of this?' Compassion identifies with the suffering of others and even makes them seem more important than concerns for our own personal aggrandizement.

God is beyond all experience

If God is 'no experience', how can we relate to God? Is the restructuring of our consciousness more important than the experience of God?
We can relate to God in and through every kind of human experience. 'No experience', however, is reserved for persons who have entered into oneness with God. Oneness with God is greater than any experience, even the most spiritual one. The restructuring of our consciousness is the path to God beyond any experience of God.

5

Happiness

There is a story about a man who had lost his keys at night and started searching frantically at the front door of his house. Another man noticed the desperate seeker and offered his help. After quite some time of searching and not finding, the helpful passer-by asked whether he was sure that he had lost his keys near his front door.

'Oh no,' the other one answered. 'Actually, I haven't lost them here but I lost them in the garage.' The passer-by was dumbfounded and cried out: 'Then why are you looking in the wrong place? Why don't you look for them in your garage?' The man answered: 'It's so dark over there; here there is much more light, which is more convenient for searching.'

This appears to be a rather foolish story. How can anyone be as crazy as that? But on second thoughts, could this story parallel our own frantic search for happiness? Are we, similarly, looking for the rare pearl in the wrong places? Father Thomas answers: 'We have a wrong understanding of happiness when seeking it in temporary pleasures rather than in the long-term transformation of character and consciousness.'

The theme of happiness and the need for a profound transformation has frequently arisen in the course of our conversations these last few days. Real happiness seems to have a spiritual connection. Can you be more specific?

The desire for happiness in every human being is perhaps the greatest proof of God's existence. Our emotional states keep changing and cannot provide true happiness. Happiness is a permanent state of mind. The lack of it creates longing for God.

> Happiness is a permanent state of mind;
> the lack of it creates longing for God

Is there a link between attaining personal happiness and the organization of society? Should our politicians be philosophers as the ancient Greek philosopher Plato suggested?

All leaders should be contemplative at least in some degree or they shouldn't be leaders; otherwise they will inflict on others their own misguided understanding of what happiness is. That is happening today in some universities, which seem to have lost all sense of discipline. The former influence of the world religions has dissipated over the last few decades, and some principles based on the innate goodness of human nature are desperately needed. The Dalai Lama is trying to instil the foundations of a morality for higher education that is based on the basic values of human nature as a whole.

You say that we want happiness but we look for it in the wrong places and when we finally know where it is to be found, our will is too weak to go for it. It sounds difficult to do.

It is impossible to do by ourselves! As the Twelve Steps of Alcoholics Anonymous affirm, you need to find out by bitter experience that your life is unmanageable. For those not addicted to alcohol or some other serious compulsion, this does not normally come about without deep meditation, daily practice or some huge tragedy that shakes you out of your ordinary ways of thinking.

> We look for
> happiness in the
> wrong places

What's most important in this life?
The main thing is to love God. There is really nothing else to do when the chips are down. To love one another is the mission of Christianity. Our human nature is very wounded. We should try to heal those wounds in ourselves and in those around us. 'The Church should be a field hospital', as Pope Francis says. People don't realize how sick they are because they carry around so many illusions about themselves. Excessive activity is a way of escaping from inner pains that we don't want to face.

Public opinion holds that success is a path to happiness. It's called the American Dream. What do you think about it?
People think that success is the path to happiness. When you don't achieve what you want, you then feel depressed even to the point of despair. Despair is the chief mistake one can fall into. God gives us millions and millions of chances to improve. Every second is a moment to be healed and to be taken over more completely by God.

God gives us millions and millions of chances

You seem to suggest that God actually works in people's lives. Can you be more specific?

God moves very quickly in some people's lives. Maybe knowing that they are not going to live too long, He acts fast. But for the average person, God works with the events of life with incredible skill and patiently brings into our lives the things that will confront the obstacles in us to His agapic, selfless love. Agape is a word that means a love that does not seek any reward and only wants to give. The greatest happiness consists in giving ourselves away. That is what the Beatitudes of the Gospel teach (Mt. 5:1–12). That is what God as Trinity is doing all the time. That is what Christ, the divine human being, actually did. The founders of the world religions usually started out with a major experience of the Ultimate Reality that took them a while to understand, but then they moved towards giving it away to others at great cost to themselves. The purpose and goal of human life is oneness with God. That is not just a goal that is fanciful. That is the way it *is*. Everything ultimately *is* one. Everything is manifesting God in its uniqueness. How can we be one with God and others in the midst of incredible diversity? Only by God's power. God is infinitely one and infinitely diverse at the same time.

> The desire for happiness
> in every human being is perhaps
> the greatest proof of God's existence

How to find happiness?

You have to change the direction in which you are looking for happiness. That is what repentance really means. You have to change your self-centred emotional programmes for happiness into true human values. Some of these are common to all religions. Each stage of human development has its own contribution to make as your relationship with God deepens. In the beginning God is a parent. Then He is a friend and soulmate, and later He is bride or bridegroom. Every relationship that you go through to mature as a human being, including the senility of old age and possibly Alzheimer's, are diminishments of the false self. They free us from our illusory idea of who we are that hinders the experience of the joy that was intended for us by God.

Is there even a meaning in Alzheimer's?

The disease as it progresses involves a loss of personality and self-identity in some people. In some cases, they don't recognize their loved ones any more and their loved ones don't know who the person they used to know and love is.

But God is working even in Alzheimer's. People with Alzheimer's are experiencing in a dramatic way what the dying process is doing, namely, withdrawing all our physical and mental powers. In dying, you lose your sight, your hearing, your taste, your feet get cold, you can't talk, you can't breathe, the heart stops and you are dead.

And then?
And then, you'll find out what life is all about! That's why we should devote more time to preparing for death than in trying to stay alive. On the other hand, the longer we live, the more chance we have of being taken over completely by the Holy Spirit. Old age also opens the possibility of manifesting God in more powerful ways. Transformed people, even if they can no longer do anything, can change the world for the better in ways that people who are acting out of their egos can never do.

> In death, you'll find out
> what life is all about

6

The Suffering of a Teacher

Suffering and disappointment crossed Thomas's path when he wanted to become a Trappist monk and had to disappoint his family. His father, Cletus Keating, was an admiralty lawyer who had built a much-esteemed law firm in New York. Holding high positions in the shipping industry, he had expected his son, Thomas, to follow in his footsteps.

When Thomas entered Our Lady of the Valley in Rhode Island in January 1944 at the age of twenty, he chose one of the most austere orders at that time: the Order of Cistercians of the Strict Observance. Before the Second Vatican Council, it held on to strict rules, such as complete silence among the monks and no family visits, not even when close relatives were dying. He recalls his beloved grandmother, who longed so much to see her grandson at her sickbed that she told a nurse: 'If Thomas won't come home to see me, will you please throw me out of the window?'

When he was thirty-eight, he was elected abbot of Spencer Abbey. The Second Vatican Council started in Rome a year later. Implementing all the changes of this Council proved to be very difficult and finally led him to resign as an abbot.

Suffering has long been misunderstood as being cultivated by Christians. Father Thomas understands it in a different way: 'Suffering tends to move us into areas of deep understanding faster than anything else, if you can accept it. Suffering that fails to teach leads to despair.'

You are revered as a wisdom teacher, so people might easily think that you haven't had any problems in your life.
How could they think that anyone can persevere in the spiritual journey without suffering? There is no way to graduate from over-identification with the false self-perspectives and habits that we all have except by suffering, especially emotional and mental pains and aches.

But did you suffer a lot?
I still do! I have almost every physical affliction an old man can have except Alzheimer's. The dying process frees us from our personality and you see more and more with the eyes of faith. According to Christian doctrine, you see what true love is, and you can't help but love everybody. Our value system after death will definitely be very different from this world's. Once the brain is dead, it can't tell us any more how we should react and what to do. You are face to face with the Ultimate Reality and with who you really are.

> Death frees us from our personality
> and you see with the eyes of faith

That sounds frightening. Is that the reason why death has always been feared? Do we judge ourselves?
It may be one of the reasons. But such a fear diminishes as love for God increases. In many reported 'near-death experiences', there is a review of the whole of one's life from the standpoint of truth, but it seems to be liberating, and not a painful 'judging' process.

People feel confident about God's forgiveness of everything in their lives. There is the realization of how much we have been protected, cared for and purified of selfishness by the all-encompassing love of God.

> Our value system after death will definitely be very different from this world's

God doesn't send sufferings; they arise spontaneously out of a world that functions on free choice and apart from God and His will.

What did you suffer from most in your life?
I can't answer that exactly because it has changed at different times in my life, and I forget lots of things. I went through the loss of people I greatly loved. I endured the folly of wanting to be a high achiever, because that's the way I was educated. This attitude tends to reinforce the pride that comes from the emotional programmes for happiness and the consequent pain of their frustration.

You apparently had a difficult relationship with your father.
It was very difficult and brought us both a lot of suffering.

Did you reconcile before he died?
I describe that in some degree in the film, *A Rising Tide of Silence*.[11] When I became a monk, my father thought I had abandoned all the values he represented and had worked hard for. In his view, I was entering a tomb. In some ways, the monastery in those days resembled a tomb. He had hoped that I would be a lawyer and follow in his

footsteps. He was a strong character, but a very good and honest man.

Did he ever understand why you wanted to become a monk?

He was very upset when I first became a Trappist, one of the strictest orders in the Church at that time. In those days, monks had no outside ministry, so it seemed to him as though we were just doing nothing, just 'navel gazing' as many monastic critics like to say.

My values were almost completely contrary to the ones my father had embraced. He graduated from Harvard law school when he was twenty and built up an admiralty law firm in New York that was held in high esteem in the shipping industry.

The monastery, of course, is a very different world. Its intense discipline helps you to face your faults, to learn about the way God acts, and to allow yourself to be healed and transformed through prayer and the ups and downs of daily life. Situations abound when you have to be obedient to superiors and give up your own will. To do what God wills is what brings real happiness. *He* is the true security, the true love and the true freedom that can completely heal the wounds of our emotional programmes for happiness.

Jesus is especially strong on servant leadership. In his view, you can't be a good leader unless you do it out of the will to serve. You have to see people as equal or better than yourself and never judge them. There are a lot of people who are tremendously generous; they don't appear in the newspapers because they do their very difficult jobs without any publicity.

If you give yourself to God, everything is a manifestation of the Beloved. You love God because there is nothing more delightful than the service of God and others, especially when it is done without expecting any return.

> You can't be a good leader
> unless you know
> how to serve

Isn't it a difficult life you have chosen?
If it is hard, it is my own fault. In this life, you are constantly encouraged by God as you bring your mental faculties into interior silence and *listen* to God speaking without words.

The end of your time in St Joseph's Abbey in Spencer proved to be rather painful. When the monks were asked in a straw poll about your abbacy, there was a fifty-fifty outcome and you resigned as the abbot. Did you leave without bitterness?
It was hard to leave because I loved the brothers, but there was no bitterness. I had to let go of the wonderful group of men that I had worked with for twenty years, as we went through all the changes of the Second Vatican Council and the revised rules of our religious order. On the other hand, resigning was a great blessing for me because it enabled me, without my intending it, to be available for the ministry of Contemplative Outreach, which was founded three years afterwards.

Suffering tends to move us into areas of deep understanding faster than anything else, if you can accept it. On the other hand, if you have no understanding of its value, it can be devastating. Suffering that fails to teach leads to despair. That's why we need to reduce everybody's suffering insofar as we can, even to the point of taking the suffering of the world upon ourselves, which is what Jesus did.

Nevertheless, leaving the Spencer monastery must have been very hard. How did you manage?
I was supported in my transition in ways that no kind of human support could provide. I did feel lonely and helpless at times. Jesus, in taking upon himself the cross, knows what that feels like. By accepting suffering, however much you may want to scream, you receive the enormous benefit of knowing God in a much deeper way than ever before.

Jesus experienced the loss of divine consolation in his darkest hour. Do you recognize that sense of loss?
God is totally giving Himself away all the time. When God became a human being in Jesus, there was no other way He could show who He was than by His passion and death. He wanted to teach us by this means who the Father is. The Father is the infinite One who gives Himself away without ceasing, first to His Son, and then to each of us. We have nothing to give back to Him *except* one thing, which is our consent to His love; to His loving us in ways that He thinks are most suitable for our divine participation.

When you are suffering from the loss of someone or something you love, you normally try to get it back; you fight for it, or you try to defend yourself. A reasonable defence may be necessary at times, but it should involve no bitterness or violence. Violence never solves anything; it just makes problems worse. Problems are rooted in our basic human deficiency of having a self that has not fully evolved into rational consciousness as yet, and still less into the divine consciousness that Jesus manifested and which will be his gift to us for ever.

> Violence never solves anything;
> it just makes problems worse

You have already mentioned that consenting to God's love is all important. What happens if we do consent?
The essence of consenting is to be transformed into higher stages of consciousness than that of rationality. The animals do what they do because of their instinctual instructions from the Creator. But humans, as we saw, have a certain freedom of choice. We can choose 'not God'; we can even choose to reject Him. We can also treat other people miserably. Since God dwells in them, this causes Him suffering by virtue of His identification with each member of the human family.

> We can choose 'not God'

The story of Adam and Eve is not a historical document, but a wisdom teaching. The ultimate cause of human suffering is that we, like them, are looking for happiness in the wrong places. In the case of Adam and Eve, it was in eating the forbidden fruit of the Tree of the Knowledge of good and evil that the devil told them would make them equal to God.

It is not wrong to want to become God, because that is His will for us. But the temptation for us, as for Adam and Eve, is to want to become God *on our own terms*. Only God's terms can possibly work.

7

After Death

When he was about five years old, Thomas became seriously ill. He overheard a conversation between his doctors and a nurse who thought he wouldn't live long. This nearness of death when he was quite young influenced him profoundly. At his first Communion a couple of years later, he made an agreement with God: 'If you let me live until I am twenty-one I'll become a priest.' Looking back on this dramatic episode in his life, Father Thomas commented: 'It was quite a decision for a youngster to make.'

This sense of wanting to offer his life to God deepened when, as a student, he recalls coming out of prayer in the Yale Chapel and feeling that he never wanted to experience anything else, that he even wanted to die on the spot. These experiences changed his focus completely from wanting to be a high achiever to giving his life to God. Father Thomas reflects: 'Our value system after death will definitely be very different from this world's.'

Was he thinking about the story of the woman who, at her death, was allowed, as an exception, to carry whatever possessions she wanted to heaven? She decided to load a wheelbarrow with all her gold bars. When she reached heaven's gate, St Peter, flabbergasted, looked at her heavy cargo and asked: 'Why did you bring all these cobblestones to us?'

Does death put an end to the transformative process that you have been describing?

Physical death is the completion of the spiritual journey in this world. It is a decisive moment in which our attachments to the world, our bodies and our personalities die. It is a leap into the unknown. What dies in death is not our uniqueness, but the attachment we have to a wrong understanding of happiness when seeking it in temporary pleasures, rather than in the long-term transformation of character and consciousness. The false self dies because it is an illusion. It does not really exist except in our imagination. The false self is built up in infancy and is the result of infantile needs and projects: specifically, survival and security, affection and esteem, and power and control.

As we saw, when one of these is excessive, we become more and more attached to it as our desires go unfulfilled, rarely gratified and never satisfied. We then become painfully discouraged.

> What dies in death
> is not our uniqueness

As we give up our attachment to the false self, we enjoy a more intimate relationship with God, and He shares more and more of His Presence. As mentioned earlier, this intimacy may develop into what is called enlightenment or awakening.

At this point in the spiritual journey, the discipline of practising patience, forgiveness and compassion is essential because we begin to see that everybody is equal and that the things that most unite us with others are our weaknesses and failures. The Christian religion teaches that God forgives us as soon as we ask. He expects our failures. We grow up spiritually as we grow up physically, passing through similar stages of infancy, childhood, adolescence, young adulthood and full adulthood. We are going some place and that's why it is called a journey, but we don't know exactly where it is or what it is.

'At death we will be transformed' says St Paul in the letter to the Corinthians (1 Cor. 15 :35–57). What will we be transformed into?

Follow the river and find the sea

Our new body will be spiritualized and not limited to its present physical presence and limitations. One aspect of creation is that, once you have been born into this world, you never die because, as the Hindu religions teach, each of us possesses deep within us an inalienable spark of divine love. That spark is the same energy that created the Big Bang. Science tells us that, in the beginning, so much energy was concentrated in that infinitesimal particle that the whole universe has evolved from it and continues to do so.

Our love for God can go on growing as we let go of our own ideas of God and let Him teach us who He is through the practice of silence and by the experience of His presence within us, around us and embracing us. It's extremely intimate, and at the same time wisdom producing. You clearly see the mistakes that so many people including yourself are making in looking for happiness in security symbols, in power and control pursuits, or in fame, prestige and success, all of which are impermanent and unreliable.

> Once you have been born into this world
> you never die

The only true security is God, whom the Eastern traditions prefer to call the Ultimate Reality. Neither term is adequate, but you have to say something to identify what you are talking about. Some words about God, while just pointers in the direction of the mystery, are better than others. One example is words that come from deep experience of the divine presence through contemplative prayer, which is a personal relationship beyond words. One falls in love with God, you might say. For people who can't fall in love because of their human disabilities, God adjusts to them and gives them knowledge of Himself through other means.

Jesus taught that in heaven there are many mansions. Does this mean that not everyone reaches the same level of transformed consciousness? Thus, in death we may not all be equal.
God, of course, can transform people at the moment of death. Still, there may be different levels of that transformation.

Heaven and hell are not so much places, but psychological states. What will make us equal despite all the differences is God's gratuitous gift to every human being to become one with Him according to his or her capacity, and to enjoy eternal beatitude.

How does one know that one has reached the end of the spiritual journey?

The spiritual journey may be divided into three stages. First, there is the discovery that there is *an Other*, and that we are not the centre of the universe. Second, we turn ourselves over to becoming *the Other*. The imitation of Christ and the visualizations in Tibetan Buddhism are about becoming what the Other is. This means integrating all the faculties of human nature into the spiritual journey through the practice of humility and the diminishment of the false self and the ego.

The final stage of the spiritual journey is the realization that *there is no Other*! You yourself are a manifestation of the divine goodness and are infinitely loved by God. Pain and joy are the same. Or rather, pain is joy without ceasing to be pain.

If one becomes the Other – God in Christian terms – one incorporates and integrates the values of the Other into one's own life. You are listening to God at the deepest level all the time and experience unceasing self-surrender. Death leads to postgraduate work in divine love and human relationships.

Death as postgraduation? Are you saying that we have the capacity to become divine?

Yes, the imitation of Christ, which is the Christian way of presenting the spiritual journey, is to identify with Christ's life, death, resurrection and ascension. The mysteries of

Christ's life are symbolic and communicate Ultimate Reality to those who are awakening. Action expands the psychotherapeutic healing process from the inner room during times of formal prayer to the whole of life. You see God more and more in other people. Even their faults don't prevent you from seeing God in them because you realize that He loves them too. The perception of the oneness of the human family, as well as consolation and desolation, come from the same infinite love that is providing us with the experiences that we need in order to be liberated from the false self and to let go of the ego. Humility is to accept the truth: to accept who we really are. Only God can bring us to that interior conviction.

The capacity for the divinization of human beings, which you referred to earlier, is already found in the writings of the early Church Fathers, for example Gregory of Nazianzen. He said that we have got the capacity to become God through Jesus Christ, just as Christ became a human being by taking on our human nature. Augustine taught that human beings could become like Christ. This sounds wonderful but is it realistic? Isn't it a project that overrates our human realities? Or is this capacity for divinization precisely what Teilhard de Chardin was hinting at?

Divinization certainly expands what we experience or expect as our human potential. But such is God's plan for each of us. God's infinite power manifests itself in our utter powerlessness. As God said to St Paul when he prayed to be relieved from the 'thorn in the flesh' that God had sent him after his ecstatic visions of the third heaven: 'My power is made perfect in weakness' (2 Cor. 12:1–10). Trust in God is what makes the impossible a reality.

How can one prepare for death?
By noticing the dark side of our personality and learning
to abandon ourselves to God's will in the present moment,
whether that is suffering or joy, work or prayer. It is to be
moved by the Spirit. In this perspective, God's will is what
happens. The Spirit manifests in us through its fruits and
gifts. The gifts of the Spirit are wisdom, understanding,
knowledge, reverence for God, fortitude, counsel and piety.
The fruits of the Spirit are charity, joy, peace, kindness,
patience, affability, goodness, fidelity, gentleness and self-
control (Gal. 5:22–3).

The fruits and gifts of the Spirit arise spontaneously as
our union with God deepens. The Beatitudes that Jesus
referred to in the Sermon on the Mount are the level of
transformed consciousness where one puts all one's trust
in God's mercy. One begins to love the opposite of the
things the false self loves, such as one's powerlessness. We
are freed from our compulsions and obsessions. Gradually
the search for gratification in sense pleasure and power
over others dissolves.

> Death is the birth
> canal into eternal life

**In our conversations, you mentioned that accepting one's
physical death is a step into the evolution of the fullness of
life. Are death and life opposites or do they belong to the
same Reality?**
Death is the birth canal into eternal life. The only thing
that really dies is the false self and the brain on which it
depends. Once the brain has ceased to exist, the true self

can make an unobstructed and totally free choice of God. To accept death is to accept God. It is the crown of all our spiritual efforts. It is the completion of the spiritual journey so that we can enter into the unveiled presence of God and see Him face to face.

You make it sound as if death can be a positive experience.
Well, it is!

That's contrary to popular and cultural opinion!
Do you want to change God or the culture? Nothing is more certain than death. It can't be simply a disaster. It's rather a transition like all the other transitions and developments of human consciousness all the way up to unity with Ultimate Reality. The latter involves freedom from the senses and our thinking processes; in other words, entering into the simplicity of the divine energy that pours itself out into the world through continuing creation. The divine energy sustains us with immense love and patience through all the stages of consciousness.

Is the transfiguration story in the New Testament a preview of something to come after death?
It's an example of the experience of contemplation. A number of the terms that appear in the text point to this. Contemplation is interior silence in progress. There is a beginning of contemplation, growth in it, perfection of it and then transcendence of it. The capacity to keep growing into God leads eventually 'to becoming God' insofar as that is possible for human nature.

Isn't that heretical?
People have experienced this incredible union in the past. It doesn't mean that we actually become God in every way, but

that through God's grace we are capable of participating in God's eternal light, life and love. St Peter defines grace as 'a participation in the divine life' (2 Pet. 1:4). Thus, we must all be part of the family of God. The whole human race is the body of Christ, the incarnation of all that God is, insofar as it can be expressed in human nature. That is not to say that God can't be expressed in other ways too. The universe is an expression of God at every level of sheer matter, embodiment, intelligence and consciousness.

8

A Cosmology

The night skies in Snowmass, Colorado, are awesome. Because of the monastery's high altitude, stars seem to shine more brightly than in the nearby cities of Aspen or Denver, which try to chase them away by their meagre party lights.

On a deeper level, this universe tells a complex and wonderful story, one about the formation of stars, the expanding of time and space, the sudden brightening of supernovae. It opens up the challenging view that creation is not a one-time event, but one that is happening continuously. Moreover, we are collaborators in creation.

Father Thomas grows enthusiastic during the interview as he talks about modern cosmology. It greatly expanded his idea of God, he says, without him needing to resort to superficial answers about science and religion. His inquisitive mind rejoices in the evolutionary theology of the eminent Jesuit palaeontologist, Teilhard de Chardin, who sees an ever emerging universe reaching towards the point Omega as Christ has a cosmic body that extends throughout the universe. Father Thomas loves Teilhard's idea that Christ is present in every particle of matter and he adds: 'God is becoming everything at every nanosecond of time and wants us to join him in that adventure.' A grand voyage in space, time and eternity is waiting for us!

What has been a source of inspiration for you on your journey?

I am inspired by the evolutionary theology and spirituality that Teilhard de Chardin preached and taught. He says that humanity at this moment in history is being called out of its limited understanding of evolution as referring only to material, animal and rational consciousness.

A new period in evolutionary history seems to be emerging, in his view, that calls us to transcend our rational powers with their desires for security and survival, power and control, and self-pleasuring and esteem, and to open ourselves completely to God's evolutionary plan. The discipline of Centering Prayer opens us to a Presence that is not accessible to rational consciousness, though it builds on it as a necessary stage in our growth into freedom. True freedom is not just freedom of choice, but freedom to do what is right, spontaneously.

That is not going to happen unless we cultivate an uninterrupted relationship with God, so that His presence is recognized in everything that happens, in other people, and in ourselves.

> True freedom is not
> freedom of choice,
> but freedom to do what is right,
> spontaneously

What is the link between the evolutionary view of Teilhard de Chardin and meditation?

The evolutionary view sees the universe, and human life in particular, as still evolving. Creation is not a one-time event, but happening every nanosecond of time. This makes it possible to relate to God and His Presence at every moment and in every place. It teaches us how to remain with God at a deeper level of our being, even when we are in the midst of intense activity or physical and mental suffering. Deep meditation is thus a unifying action, which brings together our present stage of developing consciousness and its deepest potentialities.

> It is possible to relate to His Presence
> at every moment
> and in any place

Some forms of meditation are designed to take us in that direction. For instance, Buddhist techniques are about being fully present to the content of each moment. There is a wonderful variety of meditation techniques in most of the spiritual traditions. The circumstances of everyday life are great teachers as well! We are invited to let go of our idea of God, of the spiritual journey, even of Jesus Christ, and to let God be whoever He is.

When God sees goodwill in us, He comes to help us relate to Him, including how to deal with our faults. As divine love grows, we do not so much get rid of our faults as believe that God is going to forgive them and take them away in His own good time.

> We are invited to let go of our idea of God,
> of the spiritual journey, even of Jesus Christ,
> and to let God be whoever He is

How do you see the universe?

The universe is a reflection of the divine pattern of commitment and action. Death and resurrection from God's perspective is the same thing. How does a supernova create new stars and planets? By burning out or exploding. In the latter case, new elements are formed because of the enormous heat that is generated. The immensity of these events is awesome. We are living in a universe that by the sheer force of nature has to manifest God in every possible way. We have to realize that nature has to be respected and preserved and that we are responsible for it. The planet under our care has to be available for further human evolution. Jesus wants to move humanity into higher stages of consciousness beyond the controversies that are inevitable on the rational level. We are designed to share that Oneness with each other.

The great religious traditions of the East have the same intuition. Unity is really what revelation is all about. It's not union with one thing or another, but union with everything. Freedom requires letting go, at least in intention, of the particular things that we possess, in order *to be no thing*. And when we are no thing, we are available to become everything. God is becoming everything at every nanosecond of time and wants us to join Him in that adventure.

Do you recognize this idea also in the Dalai Lama, whom you met a number of times?

The Dalai Lama gives a very special example. He is always preaching compassion and, wherever he goes, he relates to everybody he meets as if he or she is the only person in the world. In other words, he has learned to do what God does. He gives himself to everybody, respects everybody and sympathizes with everybody, without being blown away by the sorrows of the world. His confidence is that compassion will triumph in the end.

Why do you consider cosmology important?

The cosmology that scientists have produced in our times is very different from the cosmology in which earlier sacred documents and classical texts were written. You can't take these ancient texts historically as the last word. You have to take contemporary science into account. In his evolutionary view of theology Teilhard de Chardin thought that the biological level of human development was now complete. The human race has multiplied and filled the earth. It is now time for human consciousness to evolve into higher stages of consciousness and into God as the Ultimate Reality.

How has this cosmology influenced your idea of God?

It has greatly expanded my idea of God. Space and time are relative, depending on where you are in the universe, and

As your own capacity increases, God's surpassing presence also increases

how fast you or other things are moving. Our human way of looking at things is extremely limited. As you begin to lose your attachment or dependence on external things and find out by experience that God is dwelling in you and in everything else appropriately to its capacity, you realize that, as your own capacity increases, God's surpassing presence also increases.

You think of God no longer with anthropomorphic concepts which are basically childish and clearly meant to be transcended. That does not mean that such concepts are not useful for a specific person if that person does not yet have the capacity to receive the more refined insights of the Spirit. What becoming God comes down to is to know God directly, to rejoice in the healing of the emotional wounds of our lifetime, and to experience the increasing openness to oneness with everything that exists, especially other people.

Unless people can forgive, they are not going to make much progress. No one can forgive from the heart without realizing how much they have been forgiven. The capacity to do this is one of the major truths the Divine Therapist communicates through the practice of interior silence.

Do you see nature as a manifestation of God?

Nature, in its own way, is God! It is a participation in God according to its own particular level. Some spiritually inspired people say that there isn't anything but consciousness. Animals and humans are different ways in which that consciousness expresses itself, from the highest down to the smallest particles. Teilhard de Chardin said, 'Christ is in every particle'. We are each made up of trillions of particles. From that perspective, we are shot through and immersed in the divine presence through the trillions of particles that make up our bodies.

> Nature,
> in its own way,
> is God!

The mystical body of Christ is the presence of the Spirit in all of humanity. Thus everyone is a member of the body of Christ. The members have different functions, as St Paul teaches. Some build up organs or nervous systems, brains, legs, arms, blood and heart. St Thérèse of Lisieux used to say that she wanted to be the heart of the Church. Those who have had an intuition like hers express it in different ways. We also recognize the same intuition in other religions.

The interreligious dialogue has become possible in our time through travelling and the mass media. Spiritually enlightened people from all religions and no religion, through dialogue, can help each other in bringing about a more mature idea of both religion and science, and the spirituality that unites them.

On the one hand, you refer to an old tradition of silence, and on the other hand, you point to new possibilities that evolution might have in store for us. What is the connection?
Centering Prayer is a contemporary way of re-expressing traditional Christian mysticism. It is also inspired by mystics such as Teresa of Avila, Thérèse of Lisieux, John of the Cross, John Cassian, the anonymous author of *The Cloud of Unknowing* and Thomas Merton. The same silence is recommended by the monastic Fathers and Mothers of the Desert,

hesychasm[12] and the tradition of Orthodoxy, and by the great mystics of all ages.

We may be at the threshold of an immense breakthrough in the present human condition which will move people who are stuck in rational consciousness to the intuitive or unitive levels. Whatever the benefits of rational consciousness, it also has serious limitations. The chief one is that differences in belief systems lead to opposition, whereas differences from a unitive perception are meant to enrich us. One needs discernment. Other traditions have the same general faults that we have: they exaggerate some things and misunderstand other things.

It's a very positive view you give about our human condition.
How in the world did it get to be so negative? I suspect it is because religious leaders in general did not have the experience of being loved by God, which emerges from cultivating a relationship that moves into silence, stillness and then into pure awareness. The divine presence within us will then roll over and wake up inside us, revealing that all the problems of the world are very relative compared with God. Nothing really matters except God. But everything also matters because of God.

> Nothing really matters except God, but everything also matters because of God

9

On the Road Again

While reading some magazines during my transatlantic flight to Colorado I stumbled upon a story about two monks in an abbey. The older one was making life impossible for the community's newest member, ridiculing him relentlessly. As a last resort the young monk went away to meditate on the words of St Paul, 'Be transformed by the renewing of your mind' (Rom. 12:2). On his return he was, as he expected, immediately subjected to a hail of abuse. 'And after all your time away from the community,' the older man spat out, 'and all the money you spent, I still don't see you are different.' The younger man paused, made space for a few breaths, slowly pushed back his cowl, turned to his accuser, smiled, and calmly said: 'Maybe so, but I see you differently now.' [13]*

A journey can change us profoundly. Sometimes it leads us into the desert, as was the case with the Fathers and Mothers of early Christianity. Sometimes we find ourselves in a spiritual desert and experience that we can be changed and renewed on the spot by the advice of an understanding and wise teacher. Leaving our familiar situation behind in order to be able to reflect on it from a distance is part of the solution because it forces us to ask questions. What do we take with us in our luggage? What do we leave behind? How does Father Thomas look back on his journey? What does he think of his position and reputation as a spiritual leader? And how do our own journeys compare to his?

Could you summarize your thoughts regarding the basics for Centering Prayer and its particular contribution to the birth and growth of contemplation?

Ordinarily we think of prayer as thoughts or feelings expressed in words. Contemplative prayer is the opening of mind and heart – our whole being – to the divine presence within us, beyond thinking, conversing and even consciousness itself.

Centering Prayer is a method that prepares our faculties to awaken to the gift of contemplation. It leads to an intimate relationship with Christ that is beyond words, and moves into communion with him both in daily prayer and action.

This is the kind of prayer that Jesus invites us to enter in his Discourse at the Last Supper: 'However, I do not pray for them alone [those at the supper]. I also pray for those who through their preaching will believe in me. All are to be one; just as you, Father, are in me and I am in you, so they too are to become one in us.' And a little later: 'The glory you have bestowed on me, I have bestowed on them, that they may be one as we are one – I in them and you in me. Thus their oneness will be perfected . . . May the love with which you love me dwell in them *as I dwell in them myself*' (Jn 17:20–26).

This is the teaching that Centering Prayer proposes, following the whole Christian contemplative tradition and brought into dialogue with contemporary psychological, anthropological and neurological discoveries, as well as with the wisdom teaching of the Eastern religions.

In Catholic theology Jesus is not just a human being possessing a complete human nature. He is the Word made flesh, the Son of God, who in his divine nature assumed the historical human nature of Jesus. It is through the person of Jesus, the divine human being, that we are drawn to experience the Eternal Word of God, not just through abstract theological formulas, but directly.

At Jesus' baptism in the Jordan, the Father's voice rang out, saying, 'This is my beloved Son . . . Listen to him.' This listening to Jesus points to prayer as an intimate relationship with God. As listening deepens, so does the relationship with God, which gradually matures over time until we become one with Him. This is the thrust of the sacred reading of Scripture called Lectio Divina:[14] first to know Jesus in his humanity and historical life, especially in his passion and death; then to know him in his resurrection; and finally to know him in his ascension and risen life in the Trinity.

All these 'knowings' point to the reality of a growing relationship with Christ that requires different responses on our part. In other words, the focus of knowing at each level of these knowings is distinct and produces different results. To grow in divine love, through the earlier stages of relationship, is to experience an ever deeper knowledge of Christ as these stages are interiorized. They change one's perspective of God and of all reality.

Contemplative prayer embraces the term and the goal of Lectio Divina, as do all Christian prayer practices that encourage a deepening relationship and surrender to Christ. It is a movement from conversation to communion with his human and divine nature. This is to experience the oneness of divine intimacy, practised in the first century and preserved in the Christian contemplative tradition both in the West and in Eastern Orthodoxy. The contemplative life, already present within us through the divine indwelling, awaits our consent.

JUST BEGINNING . . .

How would you characterize your spiritual journey? Has it changed now that old age has set in?

I feel that I have made all the mistakes possible to make, but I keep trusting in God's infinite mercy. The spiritual journey has so much wisdom in it that I could use many more years of practice. You can do more for God at this point in your life by doing nothing than by pursuing any activity. It finally becomes clear that just *being* is more important than *doing*.

How can we do more for God by being passive than by working for Him in an active way?

We must first wear ourselves out in serving God in every way we can. As old age moves in, our capacities for action diminish, and we come to realize that just to be the human being that we are with all our limitations presupposes a greater human love than all the good works we might still do. This becomes more obvious in the dying process. All

Leading the way

that we possess and our ideas of ourselves are gradually taken away. All that is left is God's will, which is to love us into the fullness of life. This is not passivity: it requires total self-surrender.

How did you achieve the grace of divine union that you seem to enjoy?

Union with God is not a question of achieving something, or of ascending or descending some imaginary staircase. Either direction will work if you keep trying. The easiest and probably the best practice is to accept the fact that God is not 'up' or 'down', but right *here*. Right where you are! Right now! If you renew that trust again and again, you will eventually get 'there' too. Ultimately that is nowhere, which is where all creation is in the first place, including you.

How should we interpret this?

Every creature has some beauty or trust to share. If you don't perceive it, it's because you are seeing yourself, not reality.

What is it like to be recognized as a spiritual leader or teacher?

It doesn't matter whether you are famous or not. What matters is that you are you! It is possible to be an enlightened person without being aware of it. At times you might be aware that 'something' is going on inside of you. What is that 'something'? It's better not to know! Why would you want to be anything other than the person God has chosen you to be?

Looking back on your life – you are in your nineties now – how do you feel about your life's journey?

I feel I am just beginning the journey. I'd be happy to have a few more years, but at the same time it doesn't worry me, because if I die, God has other ways of completing my journey. Heaven is mostly a state of consciousness that the Beatitudes already manifest as far as that is possible in this world.

Even suffering becomes a value through identification with God and can become a source of healing and redemption for others. If we have moved beyond self-interest, we are citizens of the universe. We feel oneness with everyone, including our enemies, even if they kill us.

Powerful examples of your words are the seven Trappist monks of Atlas Abbey in Tibhirine, Algeria, who were murdered in 1996 during the Algerian Civil War. I was inspired by a saying from Brother Luc, 'I am old, ill and worn out but I am closer to resurrection than a newborn child',[15] which illustrates a complete trust in God and a new life after death. The monks were Cistercians or Trappists, like you. Do you recognize the same spiritual ethos?
One of the monks of Atlas Abbey in Tibhirine, who was murdered by Islamic extremists, prayed to God that whoever murdered him would worship God together with him after his death. In other words, he totally forgave him in advance. You don't understand that attitude unless you are moving beyond self-centredness. Inner freedom goes on growing.

> Deeper than all our faults
> is the fact that God
> dwells within us
> always

I've been seeking God seriously since I was seventeen. It has been painful at times because of who I was and my attachments to the circumstances of a well-to-do upbringing. Everybody has faults, so why be surprised by your own? Much more important than all our faults and limitations is our capacity for eternal life and happiness, and the fact that God loves us infinitely and dwells within us all the time. If you love God, you will desire good for everybody, and if you have special spiritual gifts, you will want to share them with everybody because you know they are not yours. They belong to everybody because of the oneness of the human family.

Your response to God's invitation to become God too lifts the whole human family. We need lots of people practising this love to bring society to a place where violence is no longer the response to conflict. The rational level of consciousness confronts, the unitive level unites.

ABBA, GIVE ME A WORD

Early in Christianity the Desert Fathers and Mothers of Egypt of the third and fourth centuries received many visitors seeking spiritual advice and counselling by asking, 'Abba, give me a word, how can I be saved?'[16]

In analogy with these early Christians, my team travelled a long way to Snowmass, Colorado, in order to see and speak to you as we recognize you as a profound spiritual teacher of our time. But now it is time for us to get on the road again and go back home. So, in the tradition of these pilgrims, I'll ask the same question: what word can you give us to accompany us on our life's journey?

This is a fabulous world, marvellously constructed and conceived. Nothing should surprise us. To be transformed only requires our consent. But that consent involves letting go of the ego and the false self, and letting God be God in us.

You are not just your body, thoughts, emotions or your personality, which is the chief focus of the ego. You are not even your true self when the awakening of God within you matures through the Fruits and Gifts of the Spirit.

> You are not just your body
> or your personality

Transformation takes place through the total dispossessing of everything we own, including our body, mind and spirit. God has no self. So He can be everybody with the greatest of ease and can enrich us in every way insofar as we are capable and willing. He is longing to do so. In the Christian tradition, we believe that Christ sacrificed Himself on the cross not just to redeem us from our sins and false selves, but *to invite us into an intimacy* with the divine reality that is inconceivable. To accept is to participate in God's own life, and to experience as our own, God's humility, compassion, forgiveness and utter self-surrender.

> To be transformed
> only requires our consent

PART THREE

'A Place where God can dwell': conversations with Abbot Joseph Boyle

Captivated by an Experience

'Yesterday, I saw Venus coming home,' Abbot Joseph said to me at the start of the interview. 'I don't often see this brightest of all planets because we go to bed before the stars come out. The reason is that we rise at four in the morning for our first silent meditation. But yesterday, as I was returning from a visitation to Georgia, a spectacular Venus accompanied me on my way back.'

We are a reminder to people of their own union with God

With my first question, about the planet Venus, I have obviously touched a cherished subject of the abbot. Awe-inspiring, he tells me, this beautiful cosmos we are living in and which we can call home, God's home.

Coming home is what becoming a monk has meant to him. As a teenager living in New York City, he hadn't seen a lot of stars or planets. But in this monastery situated in a spectacular valley high in the Rockies he had, for the first time, seen the Milky Way massively bright in cold clear Colorado skies. Moreover, in coming to Snowmass, he had woken up to nature and he had found traces of God in it.

At first he had some reservations in speaking about his spiritual homecoming but I was fortunate to be able to prolong my stay at the magic monastery for a few days. On my last evening, he talked more freely as the cameras were already on their cross-Atlantic way home. But my little voice recorder wasn't and he was prepared to answer my intrusive questions.

How did it happen? How was his life transformed? As a boy during a visit to his brother in a monastery, he had been impressed by the rows of monks bowing in silence at the 'Glory be . . .' and, as a consequence, he had decided to become one himself. As we filmed him doing his favourite job, driving the bulldozer on the farm and enjoying it tremendously, a deep sense of connection with the transcendent could be felt. When I insisted on a concrete answer to my question of how a life can be transformed, he replied in the most modest yet authentic way possible: 'I try to be as selfless as I can be. It's all very simple but that's how God is for me and that's what I want to be: a place where God can dwell and His love can spread through me.'

You were the first novice to come here in 1959. What was the early period like?

It was a very different era from today. The Second Vatican Council and the movements in the spiritual world made a big difference in the way we lived. When I first came to the monastery, the prayers were all in Latin whereas we now have the vernacular. There was basically no talk among the monks. We could talk to the abbot, to the novice master if you were a novice or to the one in charge of the work if the work was complicated. But otherwise we had a sign language that would cover simple situations. I was in the community with my blood brother and we only had permission to talk three times a year. For the rest, we lived in a complete silence.

Do you remember a sign from that period?

> In the Eucharist, God becomes bread

(He makes a sign with the forefingers and thumbs of both hands touching one another in a triangle.) That's God. When you put it horizontally, it's bread. If you put the two of them together, it means the Eucharist: God-bread.

Why did you join this monastery in particular?
One of the reasons I came to this community was because of my blood brother, Charlie; he was my oldest brother and he had been a naval officer in the Second World War. He was one of the founding monks of this monastery. Father Thomas was

What does the triangle mean?

the superior at the time that I became a novice, and I knew that he was a good spiritual teacher. Moreover, I preferred a small monastery to the larger monasteries on the east coast.

How did your parents react when you said you wanted to become a monk?

They were supportive, especially my mother. My dad was a bit more hesitant. His first son had become a monk, his second son had become a parish priest, his daughter was married, and then there was me, the four of us. He thought that it was enough if two of his children had a religious vocation and he asked me if I might want to become a doctor. But he never pushed me. When I said that I really wanted to pursue my monastic vocation, he agreed.

Why did you want to become a monk?

We had a good deal of religious culture in our house. We would say the rosary together every night. Every summer, if there was time off, I would walk to the church for Mass. The idea of growing closer to God was really the prime thing that we lived for.

I weighed out the possibilities of doing other things. I went to a Jesuit high school and was attracted to the Jesuit life as well, because the Jesuits are great men. But ultimately the attraction to the monastery was the strongest.

> I felt that I was standing at the threshold of heaven

I remember going to St Joseph's Abbey, Spencer, Massachusetts, to see my brother Charlie who was a monk there. I was only nine and I felt that I was standing at the threshold of heaven when I was in the chapel and saw all those monks bowing when they sang 'Glory be to the Father and the Son and the Holy Spirit.' To me it was an experience of a place where God lived. I was just captivated by that experience.

To express it slightly differently and very simplistically: as a youngster, I fell in love with God in such a way that monastic life seemed to be the best way to live that out. I pursued it as best I could and after nearly sixty years, I am still quite enthralled. I have been abbot of this community for over thirty years now. I'm reaching the end of my abbacy because, at seventy-five, the abbot turns in his resignation.[1]

Were there major difficulties you had to overcome?
I would have loved to have a wife. But I wanted this more, so I had to let go of the other option. I've chosen this life and I have been very happy with it.

What has given you most joy?
Although I can't even begin to describe it, my answer would be referring to some of those moments in prayer when I really felt the touch of God. Sometimes, a resolution to different issues comes floating in as if the simplicity of God's love is manifesting itself.

Is it an experience of the love of God?
Yes, but I can't describe it nor can I make it happen. At the time it comes in, there is a higher intensity but it doesn't happen a lot. In a less intense form it can happen frequently. God is hidden, to some extent. But He has also been a companion to me, a sort of constant presence. In that form He is not really that hidden.

You give a lot of freedom to people so that they can grow. Maybe because you feel the love of God, you can pass it on!
I really try to foster freedom and people's good sense to use it well. I have never wanted to make rulings about people's inner lives and how they are using their time. When they use their own freedom, it's worth so much more.

2

Maintaining a Faith Centre in the Valley

The monks are in this valley not because of what they do but because of how they live and who they are. What does that mean?
When I was attracted to the Jesuit lifestyle as well as to the Trappist monastery, I realized the difference between these two types of religious life. The Jesuits are people who do important things. For instance, they teach, they are missionaries, they run the Vatican observatory, while monks basically don't act in the same way.

I went to a good school and most of my classmates are doctors, lawyers or university professors while I run a bulldozer cleaning out the irrigation ditches or do household chores. So I don't 'do' anything that gives justification for the education I got.

All that I have got is what has been given to me in my life of relationship with God, relationship with all my brothers and sisters, and relationship with the whole universe.

> Lord, what do you want to do with me today?

For me, it's a question of allowing God to live in me. When I get up in the morning, I ask, 'Lord, what do you want to do with me today?' It's not going to make the headlines. I'll be doing things around the monastery and the ranch, the administration, talking to people on retreat and trying to be as selfless as I can be. It's all very simple but that's how God is for me and that's what I want to be: a place where God can be and His love can spread through me.

Your life seems to be in contradiction with 'the outside' world. People always seem to expect others to be active and productive, to justify their lives. Do you also sense the same restlessness when people come on retreat here?

The gift of this life is to invite people to think about all their activities and their running around.

What we experience is that people come to our retreat house because they are burned out. If you are not putting fuel into the system, if you're not allowing your soul to breathe in love, it's hard to keep putting love out into the world. You begin to put your ego out into the world.

Allow your soul to breathe

What we do with our retreat centre is to provide a space for people to get in touch with themselves and follow God who is at the centre of themselves in order to bring the resource of infinite God energy out in the world.

> We do nothing,
> we just are here,
> maintaining a faith centre in the valley

People keep coming back; it's really a great joy for me, even though we say we do nothing. In fact, we don't, we just are here, trying to maintain a faith centre in the valley. People can pick that up so that they are refreshed and renewed inside and, in a sense, transformed. They often go back, more centred, more acting from their heart space, while leaving behind their ego-agendas.

Nevertheless there are lots of people who reproach monks for leading a passive, contemplative, life. Is your life passive? To tell you the truth, I consider it, indeed, to be passive. When I was weighing out the decision to become a monk, I asked myself whether this was a selfish choice that I wanted to make. Was I merely looking for my own pleasure, in this case a spiritual pleasure, but a pleasure nevertheless? I started reading different spiritual authors and what convinced me in the end was the fact that there are many parts in Christ's body that don't all do the same thing.

Each one of us can only contribute a small piece to the whole picture. Even if I did some form of social work like taking care of a food kitchen, my contribution would be limited. In examining before God my own part, I concluded that by living this monastic life, I would be a reminder to people of their own union with God and of their own need of communication with God.

I want to be a token, at best, that people have a resource, that God is with them and that they can actually access that resource and lead their lives knowing that there is this inner security.

At the General Chapter of the Cistercian Order in Lourdes, you focused on identity and the question, 'Jesus, who are you and who am I?' Have you found an answer?[2]

The answer to that question is continually opening up. Before I became abbot, I was the appointed superior and I was in charge of the house because the then abbot was on a sabbatical. The atmosphere at that time was pretty low, the house didn't seem to be in good shape and some monks were depressed. On the whole, the spirit was not uplifting at that time.

> 'I am He
> who makes
> all things new'

One day after I had come in for breakfast and I was the only one – which could happen because we take breakfast individually as Trappist monks – I saw a picture of Brother Bernie who had died recently. He had been a community-building kind of person and the question that came to my mind was: 'What do I need to do in order to bring back the good old days?' When I sat down with my breakfast, this prayer came up for me: 'Oh Lord, who are you and who am I?' And I got an answer! Most of the time, it is just a form of prayer which helps me quieten down. But actually in my head I heard this voice: 'I am He who makes all things new.' It suddenly dawned on me that I was trying to bring back the old and God is the one who is making everything new. I realized that I had to turn around and look at the future. I actually started laughing by myself, realizing that I was going backwards whereas God is always going forwards!

Did you have any idea where this thought came from?
No, I don't know why I seemed to hear these words; it's a text from Scripture, which I must have heard before. The lines just came to me when I was asking: 'Who are you?' It is not as if I am constantly hearing a voice talking to me like that, although there have been some other examples as well. Afterwards, things indeed began to lighten up in the monastery. We began to get the pieces together, the mood lifted and the atmosphere became quite enjoyable.

3

Father Thomas

In what way did Father Thomas drastically change the Trappist life during the years after the Second Vatican Council?
Trappist life during the 1940s and 50s up to the Vatican Council was based on austerity, strict rules and physical silence. At that time, Father Thomas was abbot of St Joseph's Abbey of Spencer in Massachusetts where he served from 1961 to 1981.

The practice of quiet prayer or 'mental prayer' has always been a part of our Cistercian monasteries. But Father Thomas's great contribution to monastic life was to change the accent from austerity to transformation through contemplative prayer.

Of course, there is still austerity in getting up at four o'clock every morning and in our strict daily schedule of work and prayer. But the accent changed to contemplation as a transformative value that would take us deeper into the heart of God. Becoming aware of living in the presence of God throughout the day and building a relationship with God through the monastic practice of Lectio Divina and prayer in general became the focus of our life. The word 'Trappist' even became a bit old fashioned in the 1960s because of its association with austerity.

There were others as well in the Cistercian Order who had the same intuition, for instance Abbot Jeroen Witkam of the Abbey Maria Toevlucht in Zundert, the Netherlands, who started Zen retreats at his abbey and who gave a retreat here in our abbey. We invited some other Zen teachers as well in the 1970s and early 1980s who gave us retreats, or *sesshins* as they are called.

Another factor was the ever better access we had to new translations of the Cistercian Fathers and of St Bernard of Clairvaux, who wrote beautiful texts on the love of God. In that way, change was coming in from different directions.

> The monastery is about transformation
> rather than about austerity

Did you benefit from these Zen retreats?
I personally learned some very valuable life lessons from the Zen masters and the *koans*[3] during these retreats, and some of the spirit of Zen practice helped support my own Christian meditation practice although I haven't made any direct carryovers from Zen practice to Christian practice. These retreats as well as other encounters were part of the interreligious monastic dialogue that was fostered by the Second Vatican Council.

Father Thomas's contribution didn't stay limited to the monastic world. He became a renowned teacher worldwide. What happened?
Thomas's big contribution was that he took the monastic quiet outside of the monastery. He developed a method to

Silence puts you in touch with what is going on inside

quieten down and turn to prayer easily without having to become a monk. In that way, he made what was to be called 'Centering Prayer' available to every person desiring to learn it without having to become a monk.

You experienced the austerity in the days before the Second Vatican Council first hand. Does austerity bring someone closer to God or does it alienate him from his fellow brethren in the monastery?
Austerity certainly has its benefits. It can remove distraction and give some discipline to a person who is not self-disciplined enough. But by itself it doesn't get anyone any deeper into union with God.

In order to achieve this, you need the love of God and the love of the brethren, already summed up in both the first and the second commandment.

Austerity is not bad but it is not what religion and what union with God is about.

Moreover austerity by itself runs the risk that people put a priority on it. It can deteriorate and then you almost end up with the situation Jesus had with the Pharisees. They were hooked on the strict interpretation of the law, but disregarded the needs of their fellow men.

St Benedict's Monastery at Snowmass has the reputation of being a welcoming community. It could not have been easy for Father Thomas, though, to come back here after being abbot at Spencer monastery.

This monastery of Snowmass has a certain reputation for being a welcoming community. People come on retreat rather regularly. Of course, we welcomed Father Thomas, who had been the superior here before becoming abbot of the Spencer monastery. He was coming back in a way.

You were the abbot soon after. How did that go?

(*Laughs*) Father Thomas is one of the best monks! We voted for him, we wanted to have him back in Snowmass.

It was funny, though, because most of us thought he would quietly sit in the corner and say his prayers but he felt the real impulse of the Spirit that made him go out and make Centering Prayer available to a much wider circle.

He would fly out quite often to give lectures on Centering Prayer. For instance, he would fly down to Florida on Friday night, by Saturday night he would be up in Long Island for another session. On the way back, on Monday, he would stop at Detroit and then come back to Snowmass. He was on a kind of schedule of activities that a CEO of a big corporation would be worn out by. He felt that it was God's will to spread Centering Prayer and he got very active.

And was it possible to do that?
At the very time Father Thomas returned to Snowmass, Father Michael was the abbot, and four years later I was elected abbot. Both of us totally believed in him and in the mission he felt he had to pursue, so we supported him. Another monastery might have put some curbs on it.

4

Centering Prayer in an Uncentred Time

We are living in an uncentred time. Is Centering Prayer a way to get in touch with the deep mystery?
Indeed. It is a way to introduce people into that silent communication. At first our prayer tends to reach out to God with words as we bring our needs to Him. When we get quieter and more loving in our expressions of trust, we are more inclined to let go. Eventually, we have to slow down enough to hear God, who doesn't speak in any words we are used to.

We didn't have a method for this at first. The monastic way of prayer was called 'Lectio Divina'; reading Scriptures and by reading quietening down. The problem is that lay people don't have the time to sit down with the Scriptures and stay with the texts long enough so that they can evolve to prayer.

The method of Centering Prayer, based upon the fourteenth-century work *The Cloud of Unknowing*, is a good method for us today with our rather active minds. We need a sacred word to quieten us down and to help us to sit still in order to be in the presence of God without all our words and different thoughts. So, it's an effort just to be in the presence of God and communicate in silence.

Why is it so important to spend some time in silence each day?

All day long, technology is omnipresent. We put the radio on in our car; we have a CD-player, a cell phone and Bluetooth. Being in your car used to be a quiet time, and now it has become communication time.

In the morning, many people wake up to the radio, so that they can immediately listen to music or the news. People on the streets have a little wire hanging from their ear so that they can keep talking on the phone. They don't have to waste any time with being or thinking. They can keep talking from one end of the day till the other.

> We don't get to know
> our inner being

Technology has facilitated our communication enormously so that, when you have a thought, you can put it in an email and send it to a group and it is transmitted in seconds. Our world is constantly improving our ability to distribute our words and hear words from others. There are advantages to that, but what I see as the major disadvantage is that we don't get to know ourselves and our inner being. We neglect the capacity that we have to breathe deeply and allow the spirit in us, which I call God, to be active.

What does silence do to somebody?

Generally speaking, silence is going to quieten people, make them more still and put them in touch with their inner being.

On the contrary to what a lot of people think, it is not always a pleasant spiritual experience. On our monthly silent retreats, we notice that in quietening down, people see stuff inside themselves that they were gliding past, like selfishness, self-centredness.

On the first level, silence quietens you down but on the second level it opens you up to some truths inside yourself. Ultimately it takes you deeper into the communion with God by purification. Silence puts you in touch with what is going on inside yourself. It confronts you with your real motives and you can realize that you are opportunistic and ego-driven without recognizing it as such.

Is this relationship an innate capacity? Does everybody have the possibility to quieten down and to come into contact with God or are there people for whom it doesn't work?

I think it's an innate capacity. Nevertheless, some people have a greater facility with it than others; some are introverts and live more in the mind, while extroverts prefer external stimuli.

> Human beings are
> oriented to
> the ineffable mystery

Karl Rahner, a German theologian said: 'Human beings are always and everywhere, in all times and places, oriented and directed to that ineffable mystery we call God.'[4] We have that innate capacity in us. But for some people sitting in silence is unfamiliar territory and they shy away from it.

5

Purifying the Ego

Is Centering Prayer a kind of purifying of the ego?
Yes, in the course of the prayer you get deeper and deeper and the purifications are getting more and more subtle. Your original intentions are purified.

What are your most profound experiences in the retreats you have been doing?
I've had a few experiences that transported me to a silent realm, but that's not what should be singled out. I have been in the monastery for almost sixty years now and I am really happy to be here.

What has made it the most satisfying are the vigils, our early morning prayer followed by early morning meditation: Centering Prayer or contemplative prayer. Over all those years, that is the consistent practice that has refreshed me and renewed me. If I'm struggling with something, I can let go of it and move on during this prayer. The experience of going back every day to that place of being in the presence of God in an act of love and trust is more important than any extraordinary experiences.

Do you use different methods when you pray?
In addition to Centering Prayer, to which I take a slightly free approach, I also practise affective prayer and I'll use images to try to dialogue with God on trust and abandonment.

Transcend

Another form of prayer is our whole liturgy, which starts at 4.30 in the morning and which has images and texts. I do love the Mass. Although the liturgy of Mass and Communion are beautiful, it is the connection that I get out of that early morning meditation that is the strongest for me.

Prayer purifies your original intentions

Can you describe that connection? Or is it the time of day that makes one receptive?
At that time of day, 4.30 in the morning, the mind is quiet and we sit in that stillness with God with the intention to wanting to grow in that love relationship. That's the time I feel most grounded and most connected. Whatever it is that I am carrying, I can feel God lifting it and taking it up so that it is not a burden.

Can prayer achieve something in the face of an illness or violence?

I think prayer helps but it's a mystery and it can't be proven scientifically.

However, the way prayer helps is not always in the way we think about it. Once in a while, there is a miracle and there is a remission of an illness that the doctors didn't expect but that is rare. However, prayer can help people to become accepting of their situation and find God in it. A young woman who died from cancer said she was actually glad it had come into her life because it had taken her to a relationship with God she wouldn't have had without her illness. That is a transformation.

Violence escalates in its own way

When I hear about the cruelty of terrorists, my animal instincts want to strike back and approve of the use of violence. But when you listen to Jesus you get a completely different message. Violence escalates in its own way.

I was impressed by the story of the widows of the Egyptian Christians who were killed by sectarian violence. A friend, who wanted to offer his condolences, was expecting to find incredible grief and outrage. Instead, these women were sitting still, convinced that their husbands and fathers were saints and had given up their lives for Christ. It seemed to be like in the old days of Christianity when the Romans persecuted them. Inside themselves, they had come to a whole different view of things; they weren't torn apart with anger and rage and the grief of it because they could see a dimension of the presence of God working even there. That's probably strange for somebody with a secular worldview but we need to have an answer to violence.

In the film *The Passion of Christ*, which focused on the violence inflicted on Jesus, I thought the flashbacks were most touching: you see Jesus in the Sermon on the Mount saying: 'Love those who persecute you, do good to those who do evil to you.' That's the only way to change the world and Jesus is the one who has had the best answer for changing the world. Our animal instincts are not going to transform the world. Loving our enemy sounds impossible and we haven't reached this point of evolution yet, but it is the only direction that can bring hope.

What name do you give to God?

(*After a long silence*) It is not so easy to answer that question. Sometimes I use this little Trinity in my mind:

> Oh God, creator God, Father
> Oh God, redeemer-God, Jesus
> Oh God, spirit-companion-God, Spirit

To me, God the Father is the ultimate source of everything and this whole incredible universe is His gift. We, as human beings, have finally come to the point where we have consciousness and can relate to God. That's the meaning of 'the Father' to me.

Christ is the one who came to redeem us when we somehow lost contact with God because of our ego-agendas. When His love called us back, by Jesus dying on the cross and resurrecting, we are back into that flow with the Father.

The Spirit is my constant companion day by day, through everything that happens.

Can you be more specific about the way in which the Spirit is your companion?
The Spirit lifts me, in what I do, in how I interact with others even when I am not conscious of it. When people tell me something about their life, it's not as if I hear the Spirit telling me what I should tell them; I rather feel the Spirit is working through me.

I do feel that the Spirit has saved me a few times. Working on the ranch in my bulldozer is not without danger. It can roll over and the situation can get out of hand. Moreover, the machine doesn't stop immediately. It happened one day when our irrigation ditch had had a landslide and some trees had got stuck in it. While I was cleaning it out and looking from a different angle, a tree ended up pushing right against me like a spear before I was able to stop the machine. I said to myself: 'Oh, wow, thank you Lord, that was close!'

Son, all that I have is yours. You are always with me.

Have you got a sense that this work of the Spirit is deepening within you?

An introvert person gets his knowledge from introspection, but I am more of an extrovert person and I pick up a lot of self-knowledge from conversations with other people. People have often told me that they see a growth in me, that they see Christ in me. In passing this through to others, I find myself saying: 'Thank you Lord, I am grateful you're doing that. I am not always aware. As a matter of fact, I am never aware, but that is what is happening.' I can only say that I am grateful to God because He works through me like that.

What's your favourite Bible story?

The story of the Prodigal Son and the Loving Father is my favourite. Henry Nouwen, the Dutch Catholic theologian who became well-known in America for his work with handicapped people at l'Arche, Ontario, wrote a book on the return of the Prodigal Son. He points out that we identify with all three persons in the story: the father, the younger brother and the older brother.

At first I would identify with the older brother. The older brother is rather law-abiding and, as a consequence, he runs the risk of becoming hard-hearted and not compassionate. But in reading the story a second time, it emerges that I could also identify with the Prodigal Son whom God has loved. And finally, I have to reposition once more and try to be the father, who equally loves both persons.

At first in the story, it is as if the father only rejoices at the homecoming of the youngest son, but the father loves the older brother as well. The words he speaks to him are beautiful: 'Son, all that I have is yours. You are always with me.' He didn't say: 'Come on, get over your grudge!' but he voices his love for him. That's what I try to head towards in my own life here as abbot.

Another story I have always enjoyed is the story of Joseph in Egypt because of my name connection with Joseph. He was the favourite brother but he was sold into slavery by his brothers. He finally ended up being totally forgiving towards them, although his brothers were afraid that he would revenge himself upon them. But Joseph had no thought of revenge, he just wanted to help the family and see his father one more time. In my mind I like to combine the story of the patriarch Joseph in the Old Testament with the one of St Joseph in the New Testament, the husband of the Virgin Mary, the mother of Jesus.

After so many years in the monastery, you have been singing the psalms over and over again. What is your favourite psalm?
Psalm 73 is my favourite. To be near God is my joy, is the core of it. The psalm starts off in a rather sad vein. The psalmist, Asaph, doesn't understand the apparent prosperity of the wicked. Moreover he feels in spiritual turmoil himself. But then he realizes that God is with him in a special way and that's his ultimate joy.

> 'But for me it is good to be near God;
> I have made the Lord God my refuge,
> to tell of all your works[5]'

I also cherish Psalm 27, a beautiful one! It is a triumphant song of confidence and a plea from David to see the face of God. I like it a lot because it speaks about my own desire: to see the face of God.

> 'My heart says of you, "Seek his face!"
> Your face, Lord, I will seek.
> Do not hide your face from me'[6]

What words or phrases are dear to you?

Probably the one that is most repeated in my mind, when I am hiking or doing household chores, is: 'I live, now not I, Christ lives in me.'[7] My ideal is to allow Christ to live fully in me so that my self is not an obstacle to Him living in me.

> 'I live,
> now not I,
> Christ lives in me'

Liturgy is important in a monastery. What does liturgy mean to you?

When I was drawn to the monastery as a boy, I was most touched by the liturgy. When I looked down those rows of monks singing the psalms, and especially the one particular act when they bow over in a full profound bow for the 'Glory be to the Father and the Son and the Holy Spirit', it spoke to a piece of me that really responded. I felt: 'Yes, I'd like to pray to God like that. I'd like to be a worshipful person.' So, worship is very important to me.

Liturgy is perhaps bigger than worship because it builds community: we all share and give our lives to Christ and Christ gives his life to us. That's all very attractive to me as a ritual.

6

Past and Future

Looking at the brickwork of this rather hidden green monastery, I realize that monks built the monastery themselves, stone by stone. Were they trained in any way?

St Benedict's Monastery of Snowmass was really built by monks themselves. When the Abbey of Spencer in Massachusetts was built in 1950, an outside contractor was hired but the monks were the workmen. When they finished building the Spencer Abbey, they used the skills they had acquired to build this monastery of Snowmass. So, all these rows of bricks you see are laid by monks! Afterwards, they were sent to Azul in Argentina and they built a third monastery, the Monasterio Trapense, Nuestra Señora de los Ángeles.

Monks did the job of bricklayers, electricians, plumbers. I became a novice after the monastery was built and I did the manual things like washing the mortar off the bricks, painting the doors and window frames. My special job as a novice was planting trees. On one occasion – I had only been here for three days – the novice master asked all sorts of things about my character in order to accept me as a novice or not. Then, he suddenly asked if I liked painting. I answered that I preferred charcoal drawing. But he interrupted me, saying: 'No, I just want you to paint the windows!'

What about prayer times in those building times?

We always have a certain amount of manual work in our schedule, so prayer and work go together in our monasteries. In the days when we were building our monastery, there were two types of monks: choir monks and lay brothers. The lay brothers had a longer work day and they didn't have nearly as much choir prayer. It is they who mainly built the abbey and sometimes they would have their schedules changed.

Pictures from that early period show the monks as cowboys on horses driving cattle together and branding them. It is not directly associated with monks! Was it not a problem to combine being a cowboy with being a monk?

Don't forget that this is the American West! We had a cattle herd for the first ten years. There were three hundred breeding cows with their calves and the yearlings that were born the year before. On top of that we had about fourteen bulls. All together the whole cattle herd numbered close to a thousand, between calves, cows, yearlings and so on. It was quite a big ranch. Our monastery in Argentina was the same, with a big cattle herd too.

It all has become a bit more complicated in our age because of animal rights. But on the other hand, you have to obey the law and if you have cows, you have to brand them. Maybe we are lucky not to be in that business any more.

After the Second Vatican Council, a lot of monks left. How did it affect the community?

It affected our community considerably because we constantly had to rearrange the distribution of the work and do the same amount of work with fewer people.

It probably affected the atmosphere and the morale of the remaining monks as well. How did you deal with it? Did monks have difficulty still believing in the old ideal of monastic life?

I believe that all of us that chose to stay did not have trouble believing in the ideal of monastic life. The big question was, would people of the newer generation be able to dedicate their lives to living that kind of monastic life, and therefore, could the community could go on?

I can remember at the end of the 1970s, when we were so shorthanded here, as I was praying in the chapel one morning, I asked God: was it really His intention for us to stay here living the monastic life with so few fellow monks? I added: if it were His will, I would be glad to put my total effort into trying to maintain this monastic life here. When I was finishing this prayer the sense I had was that God indeed wanted this monastery to be here with its life and ministry. With that feeling of assurance I felt good about going on and contributing my energy to the life here.

That was how it was for me at least and as far as I know my other brothers must have had their own experiences that led them to stay too. Actually, after that time, I would say that morale became quite high.

The community consists of fifteen monks. Is there going to be a future for St Benedict's Monastery of Snowmass?

That is exactly the question on my mind that I have to turn over to God. At the end of the 1970s, we were down to seven, so we had gotten smaller. However, we were a lot younger and we could cover the bases a little easier than we can do now.

Stone by stone

We have twelve monasteries of men and five of women in the USA. Sadly, the reality is that two of the monasteries of men are closing. I can't say that won't happen to this monastery; it would break my heart even to think about it, but I have to think about it no matter how hard it is. Dying would be easier for me than seeing the monastery not be here, partly because so many people come on retreat and go away, with almost a new life given to them. I would hate to think of that not being available. But that's beyond me.

> Dying would be easier for me
> than seeing the monastery not be here

On the other hand, there is a growing community of retreatants. You expanded the monastery to the retreat house and hermitages, with a lot of success.

We bless the new retreat house that we built twenty years ago. Thousands of people up to this point have been doing retreats and becoming open to the presence of God. They join us in prayer and liturgy. It has been a good contribution and I would like to see it go on and to have a future long after I have died, but that is outside of my control at the moment.

Many of the Trappist monasteries have an associate programme. What about this monastery?
It indeed exists in many monasteries. People can participate with the monks up to a point and even receive instruction from a monk or a nun about the Cistercian way of life.

We, in particular, haven't gone that way because we are associated with Father Thomas Keating and the Contemplative Outreach Movement. A while back, we had 40,000 people on our mailing list. Our energy has gone into producing those retreats every month and supporting them in every way we can. It's a very similar energy to the associate programme.

What are the revenues of the monastery?
The monastery is supported by the ranch, which is an operation of putting up hay and selling it and of pasturing cattle in the summer. I love driving the bulldozer and the tractor; the sound of a diesel motor is like a cat purring to me. But everybody knows that agriculture doesn't pay the bills well.

Our retreat house is actually income producing, as also is our little book store, which is not so big but which offers a very good choice of spiritual books. Father William Meninger gives retreats outside and some of the monks practise crafts. When you add it all together we can get the bills paid and are able to go on. When we had to build the retreat house and the infirmary, we had to have a fundraiser and fortunately, people generously provided us with enough funds for that.

What do you think are the most important problems of present-day times?
As I see it, we should get people on planet earth to realize that we are one family. We all came out of the Big Bang and evolved through different evolutionary processes. I love the idea that earth looks like a spaceship when you see it from a distance. Imagine: we are all in a little spaceship in this black space and we ought to work together on it. We have to realise that we are one family. For me it is essential that we are under God's care and have to help each other.

What do you think the Church or religion can contribute to that?
I think the Church or religion can contribute very much to the awareness that we are one family and that this whole universe of ours was created by God.

It was created in love and it was created so that it could evolve to the point that the universe itself became conscious of itself. Once we realize that it was created by God and that God's nature is love, then it's our nature to love in our turn.

Nevertheless, numerous wars have been fought in the name of religions. The so-called 'new atheists' even recommend abolishing religion in order to create the perfect world. What's your opinion?

I think that they are wrong. When religion becomes tribal, it becomes a deviation from itself and produces wars. Jesus preached exactly the opposite, inclusiveness rather than exclusiveness, and the early Christians didn't even want to be enlisted in the army.

7

A Clear Sky

You are a 'nature' man. What are your first memories as a child in nature? Did you feel a spiritual connection with nature as a child?

I was born in New York and raised in the city until I was eighteen and moved to the monastery. I have no memory of enjoying the stars in the city and in fact not many can be seen in the New York sky. There were no forests or hiking trails available to me.

Truth is I woke up to nature when I came to this monastery in the Rocky Mountains of Colorado. The scenery is so spectacular: green fields with bright white snow-capped mountains in the background, whole mountainsides of Aspen trees turning gold in the autumn, and the vast canopy of stars – I saw the Milky Way for the first time!

Once I was awakened to nature by this dramatic scenery I was empowered to see the presence of God in this whole wonderful creation. As I recall, as a child my most memorable experiences of God were in a church – now the meeting place is vastly enlarged.

We're here at about 9,000 feet altitude. The sky is very clear and you're enthusiastic about astronomy. Do you have a telescope?

I always look at the night sky. But I enjoy just looking at the sky with my eyes rather than with a telescope. Somebody once offered me a telescope but I actually made a choice to refuse it. One of the reasons is our schedule. We usually get up at about 3 or 4 o'clock and we go to bed before the stars are out. Our quiet time is early in the morning and gathering the monks around a telescope at that time would be a problem because that time is reserved for our special prayer time. Moreover, it seems you always need more and more equipment in order to see more details. So, I like just looking with my eyes.

What are your favourite stars or constellations?
My favourite constellation is Cygnus the Swan, also known as the Northern Cross. It sits right in the Milky Way and it

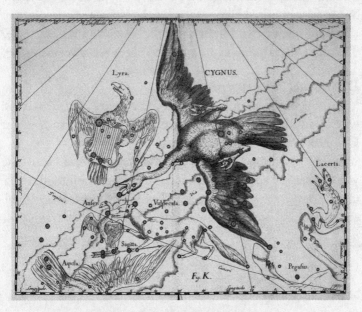

Amazed by the beauty of the stars

has a beautiful form. When I see it setting, it's like a sailboat in the sky, and the top of the mast – or the tail of the Swan – is Deneb, my favourite star. It is one of the most luminous nearby stars. It is said to be nearly 200,000 times as luminous as our sun. Its exact distance has been difficult to calculate but it is probably 2,600 light-years away. That's why it doesn't overwhelm us.

We have been talking about the inner experience of Centering Prayer and now we're talking about the overwhelming experience of looking at stars, light-years away. Is there a connection with God for you?
First of all, I believe that this universe was created by God. I am amazed at the beauty of it. Sometimes I say: 'WOW! Father, this is something.' The Milky Way is said to contain one to four hundred billon stars and the estimated guess is that there are one or two hundred billon galaxies in the universe. To realize that this is my home, God's home, is awe-inspiring.

Do you feel close to nature?
Yes, probably all monks do to some extent, even if it is by way of admiring a small flower outside. Here at Snowmass, Colorado, nature is so dramatic.

Every morning, I look at Mount Sopris. On a clear day, you can see the sun rise, hitting the tip of the mountain. On a cloudy day, you can see the clouds coming down. It is a total experience of 'awe'. I am fond of hiking in the mountains too.

8

Aspen

The city of Aspen is about twenty minutes' drive from the monastery. It is said to be a mundane city, some even call it a drug city. Do you have a lot of visitors from Aspen?

I am not sure if that is a fair presentation of Aspen. Thirty years ago, it was indeed considered to be a cocaine capital. On the other hand, Aspen has a lot of spiritual growth and a lot of people are very spiritually driven. It is in a culture of growth and it's an inspiring city in that sense. Undoubtedly, there is an enormous cash flow as well. Even so, there are lots of people from Aspen who have been coming to the monastery over all these years.

I'll tell you a story about one of our monks, Bernie, who used to go to the city when shopping had to be done. When some monks told him, 'Aspen is a sin city', do you know what he answered them? His common phrase was 'Wouldn't it be funny if they were closer to God than we are?' In that way, he silenced them. Bernie always wanted to deflate somebody's pride.

His story reminds me of the quotes in the Gospel of Matthew 'Truly, I say to you, the tax collectors and the prostitutes go into the kingdom of God before you. For

John came to you in the way of righteousness, and you did not believe him, but the tax collectors and the prostitutes believed him.'8 How do you interpret these lines?

The tax collectors and prostitutes knew what they were being given by God's love. When forgiveness comes into your life, it becomes the total focus of your life. We, like the Pharisees, often think that we lead good lives and that God owes us love in one way or another. But when the prostitutes realize they are loved and forgiven by God, they actually get a new life and have the right to go into the kingdom of God first.

> When forgiveness comes into your life,
> it becomes the total focus of your life

9

Life and Death

What is most important for you: proof or faith?
I believe that Jesus rose from the dead; I believe that the saints all live now, but I have no proof. The former atheist neurosurgeon, Dr Eben Alexander, was transformed completely after he had a transcendental near-death experience. That's why he named his book *Proof of Heaven*. Personally, I think there is no proof; it's an act of faith.

> Death is a transition

I really don't have any concern nor any fear about it. Dying has the element of transition and, finally, to seeing the face of God. I hope that, when the time comes, I can take whatever it brings. My mother and brother died of cancer so it's not unlikely that I'll develop it myself. I hope that I can go through the process graciously the whole way. Dying is not a thought that preoccupies me.

Do you expect that at your death your life will be transformed as St Paul says?[9]
Yes, I expect death to be a transition. I think it is a movement into a space that is not limited by our body and our senses that are quite limited now. I like the phrase in St Paul, that we will

'see God face to face'[10] and we'll relate to people and the beauty of who they are without the ego-agendas we have right now.

How do you imagine life after death?

I don't think much about it. I see it as infinite love, as if the whole atmosphere of heaven is filled with God as a kind of vibration going through us. I think that we are going to see and know each other in God, whatever that word means.

It strikes me on the one side as a homecoming, us returning home to where we come from, but on the other hand all of our brothers and sisters are coming home as well. There is an anthropomorphic piece to my image and I'm willing to let God do whatever He is going to do. I certainly have a very deep hope that it is a transition into an incredible related life.

> I'm willing to let God do
> whatever He is going to do

Have you got any dreams?

One of the biggest dreams I have is seeing some new people coming in and taking over the life of the monastery so that we can keep our retreat house going, which I think does incredibly good things for people.

Suppose you lived in the time of Jesus and you were one of the disciples: what would you say to Him?

I'd probably say: thank you for all that you are and all that you have done.

Us returning home to where we come from

Biography of Father Thomas Keating, OCSO

Father Thomas Keating was born in New York City in 1923.

Schools attended:

Deerfield Academy, Deerfield, MA 1937–40 (spring)
Yale University 1940–2 (spring)
Fordham University 1942–3 (graduated December)

He entered the Cistercian Order in Valley Falls, Rhode Island, in January 1944. He was appointed Superior of St Benedict's Monastery, Snowmass, Colorado, in 1958, and was elected abbot of St Joseph's Abbey, Spencer, Massachusetts, in 1961. He returned to Snowmass after retiring as abbot of Spencer in 1981, where he established a programme of ten-day intensive retreats in the practice of Centering Prayer, a contemporary form of the Christian contemplative tradition.

He is one of the architects of the Centering Prayer movement begun in Spencer Abbey in 1975 and founder in 1984 of Contemplative Outreach Ltd, now an international, ecumenical organization that teaches Centering Prayer, Lectio Divina and the Christian contemplative tradition, and provides a support system for those on the contemplative path through a wide variety of resources, workshops and retreats. He helped to found the Snowmass Interreligious Conference in 1982 and is a past president of the Temple of Understanding and of the Monastic Interreligious Dialogue among other interreligious activities.

He is the author of many books and video/audio tapes series. An extensive bibliography of his books is given on page 161.

Biography of Abbot Joseph Boyle, OCSO

Father Joseph Boyle was born in New York City on 14 June 1941 as the fourth of four children, two of whom were religious. He went to a Catholic Grammar School and to Jesuit Regis High School in New York City. Upon graduating from High School in June of 1959, he entered St Benedict's Monastery in Snowmass where he was solemnly professed in 1965. He was ordained a priest in 1970 and elected abbot in 1985.

PUBLICATIONS

Sundays at the Magic Monastery. New York: Lantern Books, 2002.
'Homilies of Joseph Boyle', in *Homilies from the Trappists of St. Benedict's Monastery.* New York: Lantern Books, 2012.

ACKNOWLEDGEMENTS

This book, curiously enough, owes its existence to the sudden closing down of the Catholic television station in Flanders, Belgium. I owe thanks to Toon Osaer, managing director of our television station, who made my last television wish come true by granting me the opportunity to travel to Colorado with a camera team.

What looked like a setback turned out to be an opportunity: an interview with a long-wanted guest on my list, Father Thomas Keating. To him, my profound gratitude is due.

I also want to thank the remarkable abbot of the community, Father Joseph Boyle. Modest yet strong, friendly but firm, he turned out to be the unexpected answer to difficult situations. I would also like to thank the guestmaster of the retreat house, Gary Dutelle, and his wife Sherry, for their help and concern.

I am grateful to the monastic community of St Benedict's Monastery of Snowmass, Colorado. The monks were welcoming to our team, although we invaded their silence and even their enclosure when filming the interviews. I would like to thank them for their kindness, generosity and continuous testimony to the mystery dominating the silent Rocky Mountains of Colorado. Moreover, as an unsuspected bonus, they provided me with the title of this book. At vespers, I heard them singing about a world without end and I was intrigued. I hope you as a reader will be too!

ACKNOWLEDGEMENTS

The film director, Dominik Vanheusden, and the camera team, Pieter Maes and Greg Poschman from Aspen, produced a captivating television broadcast of the conversations I had with Father Thomas and Abbot Joseph, which are here reproduced in print. Wim D'haveloose meticulously read my introductions and provided valuable advice.

I am grateful to Robin Baird-Smith, my publisher for five years now. From the early stages on, we discussed this challenging project. His publisher's skills got me through the rough parts of it. He has become a friend since the publication of my first book under his care, *The Dominican Way*. In addition I would like to thank Jamie Birkett, the editor at Bloomsbury, for guiding this book through all the stages of the publishing process.

I am especially grateful to my beloved husband, Gerard Bodifee, the most important person in my life. As an author and astronomer, he coached me on the interests that we shared with Father Thomas Keating: cosmology, science, Teilhard de Chardin, Christianity. Late at night, I called him long distance from Colorado to ask details about the star constellations in the Rockies, and in the morning I picked up the subject with Father Joseph Boyle, who shared my husband's love for the stars.

All these people helped me in their own specific ways to find an answer to the question about the meaning of life, which led me to Colorado in the first place. On this quest, my husband is my inspiring companion.

Lucette Verboven

NOTES

INTRODUCTION: A JOURNEY

1 George Herbert, 'Love' in *The Norton Anthology of English Literature* (New York: W. W. Norton & Company Inc.: 1962), p. 1267.

2 *Eeuwigheid en Stilte*, ed. Meinhard van de Reep, trans. Lucette Verboven (Heemstede: Altamira, 1992), p. 50.

3 Lucette Verboven, *Pelgrim in het leven* (Kapellen/Heeswijk: Pelckmans/Dabar-Luyten, 1999), and on www.lucetteverboven.be.

4 Aldous Huxley, *Music at Night and Other Essays* (North Stratford: Ayer Company Publishers, 2000).

5 *Lucette Verboven meets Jordi Savall in Bruges, Belgium. Braambos* broadcast. Article in *Tertio*, 14 February 2007.

6 Tavener wrote the song as a tribute to Athene Hariades, a Greek girl who died in a cycling accident.

7 *Lucette Verboven meets Sir John Tavener in Dorset, UK. Braambos* broadcast. Article in *Tertio*, 14 March 2007.

8 'Grow slack': i.e. wanting to go back.

9 'What do ye lack?' or 'What do you want?' was the typical question asked when a customer entered a shop or a pub in the seventeenth century.

10 Gerard Bodifee in *Het Mooiste Woordenboek*, trans. Lucette Verboven (Schoten: Het Bronzen Huis), p. 49.

11 *Sundays at the Magic Monastery: Homilies from the Trappists of St. Benedict's Monastery* (New York: Lantern Books, 2002).

12 Thomas Keating, *Invitation to Love* (London: Bloomsbury, 2014), p. 64. Read the story about Bernie in the conversation with Abbot Joseph hereafter.

13 Theophane the Monk, *Tales of a Magic Monastery* (New York: Crossroad, 1981).

14 John 1:14.

CONVERSATIONS WITH FATHER THOMAS KEATING

1 Leo Tolstoy, *The Kingdom of God is Within You* (London: Walter Scott, 1894).

2 Dante Alighieri, *La Divina Commedia* (Milan: Fabbri Editori, 1992), opening verses trans. Lucette Verboven.

3 After discovering the fourteenth-century classic *The Cloud of Unknowing*, Fr William Meninger had started teaching this 'Prayer of the Cloud' to priests at the retreat house.

4 Fr Basil Pennington published his bestselling book *Centering Prayer* in 1980, and spread the practice through lectures and workshops. He died from the consequences of a car accident in 2005.

5 The term 'Centering Prayer' was suggested by the participants of the first retreat given to a lay audience by Fr Basil Pennington in Connecticut, although the term was used by Thomas Merton previously.

6 Evagrius Ponticus, one of the most influential theologians of the fourth century, became a monk in the Egyptian desert.

7 Thomas Keating, *St Thérèse of Lisieux: A Transformation in Christ* (New York: Lantern Books, 2000).

8 Negative or apophatic theology is an attempt to refer to God by negation because experiences of God are beyond the realm of language or concepts. This tradition is often balanced by positive or cataphatic theology, which describes God through specific attributes such as love or mercy, and through revelation and incarnation.

9 Bernard of Clairvaux, *In Praise of the New Knighthood*, trans. M. Conrad Greenia (Kalamazoo, MI: Cistercian Publications, 2000); *Tempeliers*, trans. Guerric Aerden OCSO, Rik Van Nieuwenhove (Budel: Damon, 2015), p. 104.

10 Lucette Verboven, *The Dominican Way* (London/New York: Bloomsbury/Continuum, 2011), p. 189.

11 *A Rising Tide of Silence*, film about Father Keating's life, Temple Rock, directed by Elena Mannes and Peter Jones, 2014.

12 Term used in the Eastern Orthodox Church for the practice of inner prayer, aimed at union with God on a level beyond images, concepts and language.

13 Fr Daniel O'Leary, *The Tablet*, London, 2015.

14 The Benedictine practice of reading, meditating, praying and contemplating Scripture, not as texts to be studied but as a way of experiencing the Living Word.

15 Luc Dochier, known as Frère Luc, took care as a doctor of the local people at the Abbey of Our Lady of Atlas. 'I am old, ill and worn out. I have seen much without becoming cynical. After all, I know that I am closer to resurrection and life than a newborn child, and that fills me with great joy. I carry on' (2 August 1993). *Extraits de lettres de frère Luc, Chemins de Dialogue, Revue théologique et internationale sur le dialogue interreligieux*, no. 27, trans. Lucette Verboven (*L'écho de Tibhirine*, Marseille, 2006).

16 John Chryssavgis, *In the Heart of the Desert: The Spirituality of the Desert Fathers and Mothers* (Bloomington, IN: World Wisdom, 2008), p. 155.

CONVERSATIONS WITH ABBOT JOSEPH BOYLE

1 Joseph Boyle was re-elected as abbot in September 2016.

2 *Address to the General Chapter at Lourdes in the Year 2000* in *The Cistercian Studies Quarterly*, 35:3 (2000), pp. 279–81.

3 A *koan* is a question or a story which aims at provoking the great breakthrough, leading to spiritual enlightenment.

4 Karl Rahner: 'My ultimate purpose, in all that I have written, is but to say this one simple thing to my readers – whether they know it or not, whether they reflect on it or not, human beings are always and everywhere, in all times and places,

oriented and directed to that ineffable mystery we call God',
in Karl Rahner im Gespräch, Band, 1: 1964–77, ed. Paul
Imhof and Hubert Biallowons (Munich: Kösel Verlag, 1982),
trans. Lucette Verboven p. 301.

5   Ps. 73:28–30.
6   Ps. 27:8–9.
7   Gal. 2:20.
8   Mat. 21:31–2
9   'Behold, I tell you a mystery. We shall not all fall asleep,
but we will all be changed, in an instant, in the blink of an
eye, at the last trumpet. For the trumpet will sound, the
dead will be raised incorruptible, and we shall be changed.'
United States Conference of Catholic Bishops, *USCCB Bible*,
1 Cor. 15:51–3.
10 1 Cor. 13:12.

BIBLIOGRAPHY

BOOKS BY THOMAS KEATING OCSO

Finding Grace at the Center (with Basil Pennington and Thomas E. Clark). Petersham, MA: St Bede's Publishing, 1978.
The Heart of the World. New York: Crossroad Publishing, 1981.
And the Word Was Made Flesh. New York: Crossroad Publishing, 1983.
Open Mind, Open Heart: The Contemplative Dimension of the Gospel. New York: Continuum Publishing, 1986.
Awakenings. New York: Crossroad Publishing, 1991.
The Mystery of Christ: The Liturgy as Spiritual Experience. New York: Continuum Publishing, 1991.
Invitation to Love: The Way of Christian Contemplation. New York: Continuum Publishing, 1992.
Reawakenings. New York: Crossroad Publishing, 1992.
The Kingdom of God is Like . . . New York: Crossroad Publishing, 1993.
Intimacy with God. New York: Crossroad Publishing, 1994.
Active Meditations for Contemplative Prayer. Compiled by Grace Padila. New York: Continuum Publishing, 1995.
Crisis of Faith, Crisis of Love. New York: Continuum Publishing, 1995.
Centering Prayer in Daily Life and Ministry, with Basil Pennington, co-edited with Gustave Reininger. New York: Bloomsbury Academic, 1997.
The Diversity of Centering Prayer. New York: Bloomsbury Academic, 1998.
Heart of the World: Spiritual Catechism. New York: Crossroad Publishing, new edn, 1999 [1st edn 1988].

The Human Condition: Contemplation and Transformation (Wit Lectures – Harvard Divinity School). Mahwah, NJ: The Paulist Press, 1999.

Journey to the Center: A Lenten Passage. Compiled by Therese Johnson Bracherd. New York: Crossroad Publishing, 1999.

The Better Part: Stages of Contemplative Living. New York: Continuum Publishing, 2000.

Fruits and Gifts of the Spirit. New York: Lantern Books, 2000.

St. Thérèse of Lisieux: A Transformation in Christ. New York: Lantern Books, 2000.

Divine Indwelling: Centering Prayer and Its Development. Essays of Father Thomas Keating and Others. New York: Lantern Books, 2001.

Foundations for Centering Prayer and the Christian Contemplative Life: Open Mind, Open Heart, Invitation to Love, Mystery of Christ. New York: Continuum/Bloomsbury, 2002.

Sundays at the Magic Monastery: Homilies from the Trappists of St. Benedict's Monastery (with Thomas Keating, William Meninger, Joseph Boyle and Theophane Boyd). New York: Lantern Books, 2002.

The Transformation of Suffering: Reflections on September 11 and the Wedding Feast at Cana in Galilee. New York: Lantern Books, 2002.

Active Prayer: On Retreat with Father Thomas Keating. New York, Continuum Publishing, 2005.

Centering Prayer: On Retreat with Father Thomas Keating. New York, Continuum Publishing, 2005.

Lectio Divina: On Retreat with Father Thomas Keating. New York, Continuum Publishing, 2005.

Manifesting God. New York: Lantern Books, 2005.

Welcoming Prayer: On Retreat with Father Thomas Keating. New York, Continuum Publishing, 2005.

The Daily Reader for Contemplative Living: Excerpts from the Works of Father Thomas Keating, OCSO: Sacred Scripture, and Other Spiritual Writings, ed. Stephanie Iachetta. New York: Bloomsbury Academic, 2009.

Divine Therapy and Addiction: Centering Prayer and the Twelve Steps. New York: Lantern Books, 2009.

Meditations on the Parables of Jesus. New York: Crossroad Publishing, new edn, 2010.

And the Word Was Made Flesh. New York: Lantern Books, 2011.

Reflections on the Unknowable. New York: Lantern Books, 2014.

Consenting to God as God is. New York: Lantern Books, 2016. (Collection of Miami Meetings between January 2007 and April 2009, with members of the council of the Spanish and Portuguese branch of Contemplative Outreach.)

A NOTE ON THE TYPE

The text of this book is set in Adobe Caslon, named after the English punch-cutter and type-founder William Caslon I (1692–1766). Caslon's rather old-fashioned types were modelled on seventeenth-century Dutch designs, but found wide acceptance throughout the English-speaking world for much of the eighteenth century until replaced by newer types towards the end of the century. Used in 1776 to print the Declaration of Independence, they were revived in the nineteenth century and have been popular ever since, particularly amongst fine printers. There are several digital versions, of which Carol Twombly's Adobe Caslon is one.